THE BEATLES

THE BEATLES
A Musical Biography

Kate Siobhan Mulligan

THE STORY OF THE BAND
CHRIS SMITH, SERIES EDITOR

GREENWOOD

AN IMPRINT OF ABC-CLIO, LLC
Santa Barbara, California • Denver, Colorado • Oxford, England

Library of Congress Cataloging-in-Publication Data

Mulligan, Kate Siobhan.
   The Beatles : a musical biography / Kate Siobhan Mulligan.
      p. cm. — (Story of the band)
   Includes bibliographical references and index.
   ISBN 978-0-313-37686-3 (alk. paper) — ISBN 978-0-313-37687-0
(ebook) 1. Beatles. 2. Rock musicians—England—Biography. I. Title.
  ML421.B4M85   2010
  782.42166092'2—dc22
  [B]   2010014752

ISBN: 978-0-313-37686-3
EISBN: 978-0-313-37687-0

14 13 12 11 10   1 2 3 4 5

This book is also available on the World Wide Web as an eBook.
Visit www.abc-clio.com for details.

Greenwood
An Imprint of ABC-CLIO, LLC

ABC-CLIO, LLC
130 Cremona Drive, P.O. Box 1911
Santa Barbara, California 93116-1911

This book is printed on acid-free paper ∞

Manufactured in the United States of America

Contents

Series Foreword

Green Day! The Beatles! U2! The Rolling Stones! These are just a few of the many bands that have shaped our lives. Written for high school students and general readers, each volume in this exciting series traces the life of a band from its beginning to the present day. Each examines the early life and family of band members, their formative years and inspirations, their career preparation and training, and the band's awards, achievements, and lasting contributions to music.

Designed to foster student research, the series has a convenient format. Each book begins with a timeline that charts the major events in the life of the band. The narrative chapters that follow trace the birth, growth, and lasting influence of the band across time. Appendices highlight awards and other accomplishments, while a selected bibliography lists the most important print and electronic resources for high school student research—or for anyone just interested in learning more about the band.

These books also help students learn about social history. Music, perhaps more than any other force, has shaped our culture, especially in recent times. Songs comment on the events of their era and capture the spirit of their age. They powerfully touch the lives of listeners and help people—especially young people—define who they are.

So too, the lifestyles of band members reflect larger social trends and promote and provoke reactions within society. By learning about the bands, students also learn more about the world they live in.

So have a seat, settle in, and crank up the volume!

Acknowledgments

Thanks to my husband, Peter, for putting up with my library fees and reclusiveness, and for making dinner for himself during the writing of this book. Thanks to my parents for raising me right: to my father, for teaching me about the wonderful and addictive world of music; and to my mother for all the lunches, dinners, and love in between chapters. Thanks to my friends for putting up with my antisocial lifestyle. Thanks to Maryanne, whose love for the Beatles encouraged me endlessly, and who willingly read and reread all my mistakes. Thanks to the tireless editors at Greenwood and ABC-CLIO, especially Chris Smith: thanks for convincing me I could do this. And thanks to the Beatles for being the Beatles.

Shortly after gaining Ringo, the group signed a contract with EMI and recorded their first big hit, "Love Me Do," in October of 1962. It had good success, rising into the Top 20. Their next song, called "Please Please Me," which eventually rose to the number one spot in the United Kingdom, was released in January of 1963. The life of the band was hectic; John even missed the birth of his first son, Julian, in April of 1963, and hardly ever saw his wife, Cynthia, whom he had married in 1962. They toured nonstop around the United Kingdom, and when they weren't touring, they were back in the studio to record more hits. That year they released four singles and two albums in the United Kingdom, *Please Please Me,* and *With the Beatles.*

In 1964, the band made their first trip to America, after which nothing would ever be the same. They arrived on February 7, to be greeted by 5,000 screaming girls on the roof of the airport in New York. Never before had such a welcome been waiting for anyone, not even kings or queens. "Beatlemania," as it was called, had struck America hard, and everywhere the Beatles went was flooded with thousands of screaming girls, who had gone crazy over the band's unique style: most notably, the Beatles' long, "mop-top" hair—which was socially unacceptable at the time—that hung in their eyes and shook about as they sang. During their trip to New York, they would win over reporters by giving witty interviews, with quick come-backs and funny antics; as well, their funny Liverpool accent was hard not to like. During this trip, they appeared on *The Ed Sullivan Show* and were watched by a record-breaking 70 million viewers. The Beatles unleashed their songs on America, all of which rocketed straight to number one with sales that no one could have predicted, and the likes of which had never been seen before: in April of 1964, the Beatles held the top five spots on the Billboard Top 100. Not only had that never been done before, nor since, but it was also amazing that a British band had conquered America, making way for what would be called "The British Invasion." They would return to America in August for a proper tour, selling out shows in every single city. In 1964, they released four more singles, a whole slew of albums (mostly re-releases in the United States), and a movie called *A Hard Day's Night.*

Only more mayhem awaited the band in 1965. They returned to America that summer and played a historic concert at Shea Stadium in New York, with more than 55,000 people in attendance. Until then, no band had ever played a stadium, let alone sold out a show there. It was the largest audience in history at the time. During this tour, they were introduced to Bob Dylan, who in turn introduced the group to marijuana, thus changing the course of music forever. That year they released three more singles, two more albums (*Help!* and *Rubber Soul*, which was their first album influenced by drugs), and another movie, called *Help!* To cap off another huge year, they received an award from Queen Elizabeth, called an MBE (Member of the British Empire), which caused quite a stir, as the award was usually given to war heroes.

The following year, 1966, was the last year the Beatles world tour. In Japan, a terrorist group threatened the band for disturbing their culture, so they were confined to their hotels the entire stay. In the Philippines, the Beatles accidentally "snubbed" the president's wife and did not appear at a party she was having, and the whole country seemingly turned on them; they barely made it out of the country in one piece. The most famous scandal, however, was when a quote by John was reprinted in American in which he said that the Beatles were more famous than Jesus himself—a quote that did not sit well with the highly religious southern states. Albums were publicly burned, radios banned their music, and even the Ku Klux Klan threatened the well-being of the Beatles should they decide to return. Of course, they did return that summer, as they had already booked their tour. John attempted to reconcile with the press, apologizing for the misunderstanding, but to little avail. After a wild tour through America, playing each and every night, and in light of the mayhem they'd faced in the Philippines, the Beatles swore off touring for good and played their last show in Candlestick Park, San Francisco, on August 29, 1966. The year ended with three more singles and a new album, *Revolver*. If *Rubber Soul* was their "pot" album, then *Revolver* was their "acid" album, influenced by a new drug, better known as LSD, which had been taking over London. It would change their music and practically reinvent the band.

Though they stopped touring in 1966, they continued to make music, music that would define a generation and change the face of rock 'n' roll forever. They released the acid-soaked album, *Sgt. Pepper's Lonely Hearts Club Band*, which would be the backdrop to 1967's "Summer of Love" and the rise of the hippie movement. In June, they played their new song, "All You Need Is Love," on television, and it was watched by 500 million people in more than two dozen countries. Sadly, in August of 1967, Brian Epstein, their faithful manager, died after accidentally overdosing on sleeping pills over the course of a few days. Without Brian's voice to guide them, the Beatles began to make their own decisions, which proved ill-fated. One example was Paul's idea of the *Magical Mystery Tour*, in which the Beatles toured around England on a bus, filming a variety of scenes and releasing the footage as an acid-soaked album and movie that year. It would be their first failure. Another big mistake was the formation of Apple, the Beatles' company, which they hoped to use to further other artists' work. The first endeavor was a clothing store that lost them more than £200,000 in just half a year.

In 1968, the Beatles took a trip to India to study spirituality and meditation under a guru called Maharishi Mahesh Yogi, or simply the Maharishi. During this time they stopped using drugs and wrote dozens of songs that would go on to be their next album, officially called *The Beatles*, but widely known as the *White Album* due to its all-white cover. The *White Album* consisted of more than 30 songs and was one of the first double albums ever released; it would go on to be the best-selling double album of all time. Also this year, John would publicly divorce his wife of eight years, Cynthia, to pursue a relationship with a Japanese avant-garde artist named Yoko Ono. The two began staging "happenings," slang for nonviolent protests, mostly against America's role in the Vietnam War.

It was the beginning of the end in 1969. The band fought all the time, mainly over Paul's overbearing "leadership" of the band, often telling the others what to do or how to play; as well, John brought Yoko into the recording studio with him, causing immeasurable amounts of tension among the Beatles. Apple was losing money rapidly, so they decided to release a "live" album, where all the songs were recorded in one take, rather than pieced together; thus, they could send a concert to their fans, rather than have to go on tour. This came to a head when the Beatles famously performed live from the roof of the Apple building, a moment that would be copied by other bands for years to come. However, the music they recorded for what would be known as *Let It Be* was largely inaudible and sounded poor. They shelved the idea for the time being and began working on a completely opposite project: recording an album they way they used to, with professional editing and layering of the music. Knowing it might be their last album, they put their differences aside and recorded possibly the best work of their career: *Abbey Road*, named after the recording studio that had made them so famous. It was released October 1, 1969, and went straight to number one, just as had everything else the band released.

Little did fans know that it was the end. In a series of lawsuits beginning in 1968, the Beatles had essentially lost the rights to their music, had lost unbelievable amounts of money through Apple, and had lost the energy to go on any further. The band had irreconcilable differences that drove them apart: John was rock, and Paul was pop; George was sick of being overshadowed, and Ringo felt unneeded. John had announced to the band that he was quitting in 1969, but it was Paul who announced it publicly on April 10, 1970. *Let It Be* was finally released that year and went straight to number one, along with a film of the Beatles recording, which also had great success. With that, the four lads from Liverpool parted ways.

Overall, the Beatles had 17 number one hits in the United Kingdom and 20 number one hits in the United States, and 13 official albums (that is, not rereleases or compilations), all of which had unbelievable success. They defined a generation and led a musical revolution; they pushed the boundaries and rules of music and defied social expectations. They paved the way for many more bands to come and are thus hailed as the cornerstone of rock 'n' roll. Beyond 1970, Paul had great success with his band Wings, and George and Ringo had strong solo careers. John continued to be a peace activist with Yoko, whom he married, and continued making music until the day he was unfortunately shot by a fan on December 8, 1980. He has been immortalized as a rock legend, a musical genius, and a revolutionary activist. George passed in 2001, leaving behind a successful solo career. Paul and Ringo continue to make music and keep the Beatles' legend alive. With four of the Beatles' albums in the Top 10 of *Rolling Stone Magazine*'s "Greatest Albums of All Time," and four more in the Top 100, the legacy of the Beatles continues to this day.

Timeline

September 19, 1934	Brian Epstein, manager of the Beatles, is born.
July 7, 1940	Ringo Starr is born.
October 9, 1940	John Lennon is born.
June 28, 1942	Paul McCartney is born.
February 25, 1943	George Harrison is born.
March 1957	John and Pete Schotton form the Quarrymen.
July 6, 1957	Paul and John meet.
August 7, 1957	The Quarrymen perform at the Cavern for the first time.
February 6, 1958	Paul introduces George to John.
July 15, 1958	John's mother is killed in a car accident.
August 29, 1958	The Quarrymen play the Casbah for the first time.
January 1960	Stu Sutcliffe joins the band.
May 1960	The Quarrymen change their name to the Beatals, and then to the Silver Beetles.
June 1960	The Silver Beetles become the Beatles.
August 12, 1960	Pete Best joins the band.
August 16, 1960	The Beatles leave for Hamburg, Germany.
February 9, 1961	The Beatles perform at the Cavern Club.
November 9, 1961	Brian Epstein goes to hear the Beatles play.

1962

January 1	The Beatles audition for EMI in London.
February 13	Brian Epstein meets with George Martin after being turned down by EMI.
June 6	The Beatles audition for George Martin and are offered a record deal.
August 15	Ringo Starr accepts an offer to drum for the Beatles.
August 16	Pete Best is fired as their drummer.
August 23	John marries his girlfriend, Cynthia Powell.
September 4	The Beatles record for the first time at Abbey Road Studios.
October 1	The Beatles sign a formal contract with Brian Epstein.
October 5	"Love Me Do" / "PS I Love You" is released.
December 31	The Beatles play their final show in Hamburg, Germany.

1963

January 11	"Please Please Me" / "Ask Me Why" is released.
January 19	The Beatles have their TV debut on *Thank Your Lucky Stars*.
February 11	The Beatles record their first album, *Please Please Me*.
February 22	*Please Please Me* is number one on the charts.
April 8	Cynthia gives birth to a son, Julian.
April 11	"From Me To You" / "Thank You Girl" is released.
April 18	Paul meets Jane Asher.
August 3	The Beatles play their last show at the Cavern.
August 23	"She Loves You" / "I'll Get You" is released.
October 13	The Beatles appear on *Sunday Night at the Palladium*.
November 4	The Beatles perform for the British royal family.
November 9	Northern Songs, John and Paul's company, is formed.
November 22	Their second album, *With the Beatles*, is released.

1964

January 20	*Meet The Beatles* is released in the United States.
January 25	"I Want To Hold Your Hand" goes to number one.
January 30	"Please Please Me" / "From Me To You" is released in the United States.

February 7	*All My Loving* is released in the United Kingdom.
	The Beatles arrive in New York City to be greeted by 5,000 fans.
February 9	The Beatles perform on *The Ed Sullivan Show*, watched by 70 million people.
March 2	"Twist and Shout" / "There's a Place" is released in the United States.
	Shooting for *A Hard Day's Night* begins.
March 16	"Can't Buy Me Love" / "You Can't Do That" is released in the United Kingdom.
March 23	"Do You Want To Know A Secret" / "Thank You Girl" is released in the United States.
April 4	The Beatles assume the top five positions on the American charts.
April 23	*The Second Beatles' Album* is released in the United States.
April 27	"Love Me Do" / "PS I Love You" is released in the United States.
June 4	The Beatles embark on their world tour.
June 10	*A Hard Day's Night* is released in the United Kingdom (June 26 in the United States).
July 10	"A Hard Day's Night" / "Things We Said Today" is released in the United Kingdom.
July 13	"A Hard Day's Night / "I Should Have Known Better" is released in the United States.
July 20	"I'll Cry Instead" / "I'm Happy Just to Dance With You" is released in the United States.
	"And I Love Her" / "If I Fell" is released in the United States.
August 18	The Beatles embark on their first official American tour.
September 17	The Beatles are paid $150,000 to play in Kansas.
November 23	*The Beatles' Story* is released in the United States.
	"I Feel Fine" / "She's A Woman" is released in the United States.
December 4	*Beatles for Sale* is released in the United States.
December 15	*Beatles' 65* is released in the United States.

1965

February 11	Ringo marries girlfriend Maureen Cox.
February 15	"Eight Days A Week" / "I Don't Want To Spoil the Party" is released in the United States.

February 22	The Beatles go to the Bahamas to begin filming *Help!*
April 9	"Ticket To Ride" / "Yes It Is" is released in the United Kingdom (April 19 in the United States).
June 4	*Beatles for Sale (No. 2)* is released in the United Kingdom.
July 29	*Help!* the movie premieres in the United Kingdom.
August 6	*Help!* the album is released in the United Kingdom (August 13 in the United States).
August 15	The Beatles return to America and play Shea Stadium to an audience of over 55,000 people, the largest concert attendance ever at the time.
August 27	The Beatles meet Elvis.
September 13	Ringo has a son, Zak.
	"Yesterday" / "Act Naturally" is released in the United States.
October 26	The Beatles receive their MBEs from the queen.
December 3	"We Can Work It Out" / "Daytripper" is released in the United Kingdom (December 6 in the United States).
	Rubber Soul is released in the United Kingdom (December 6 in the United States).

1966

January 21	George marries girlfriend Pattie Boyd.
February 21	"Nowhere Man" / "What Goes On" is released in the United States.
March 4	*The London Evening Standard* prints an article in which John states that the Beatles "are more popular than Jesus."
May 30	"Paperback Writer" / "Rain" is released in the United States (June 10 in the United Kingdom).
June 20	*Yesterday … and Today* is released in the United States.
June 24	The Beatles begin another world tour.
July 5	The Beatles encounter backlash in the Philippines.
July 29	American teen magazine *Datebook* reprints John's quote about being more popular than Jesus.
August 5	"Eleanor Rigby" / "Yellow Submarine" is released in the United Kingdom (August 8 in the United States).

August 11	The Beatles return to America for another tour; John attempts to apologize at press conferences.
August 29	The Beatles play what will be their last official live concert in San Francisco.
November 9	John meets an artist named Yoko Ono.

1967

January 27	The Beatles sign a new seven-year contract with EMI.
February 13	"Strawberry Fields Forever" / "Penny Lane" is released in the United States (February 17 in the United Kingdom).
May 15	Paul meets photographer Linda Eastman.
May 26	*Sgt. Pepper's Lonely Hearts Club Band* is released in the United Kingdom (June 2 in the United States).
June 25	The Beatles perform "All You Need Is Love" on satellite TV, watched by over 500 million people.
July 7	"All You Need Is Love" / "Baby You're a Rich Man" is released in the United Kingdom (July 17 in the United States).
August 19	Ringo and Maureen have their second son, Jason.
August 25	The Beatles and their wives head to Bangor, Wales, to attend a weekend conference by the Indian guru, known as the Maharishi.
August 27	Brian Epstein is found dead in his bedroom.
September 11	The Beatles embark on the Magical Mystery Tour.
November 24	"Hello, Goodbye" / "I Am The Walrus" is released in the United Kingdom (November 27 in the United States).
November 27	The *Magical Mystery Tour* album is released in the United States.
December 7	The Beatles' Apple Boutique opens.
December 26	*Magical Mystery Tour* airs on television.

1967

February 15	The Beatles leave for India.
March 15	"Lady Madonna" / "The Inner Light" is released in the United Kingdom (March 18 in the United States).
May 11	John and Paul go to America to announce the opening of Apple Corps.

May 22	John and Yoko Ono appear publicly together.
June 21	Apple Corps moves to 3 Savile Row.
July 17	The Beatles' animated movie, *Yellow Submarine*, premiers in London.
July 31	The Beatles' Apple Boutique closes.
August 22	Cynthia sues John for divorce on grounds of his adultery with Yoko Ono.
August 26	"Hey Jude" / "Revolution" is released in the United States (August 30 in the United Kingdom).
November 8	John and Cynthia are divorced.
November 11	John and Yoko's first album, *Unfinished Music No. 1—Two Virgins*, is released in the United States (November 29 in the United Kingdom).
November 22	*The Beatles* is released in the United Kingdom (November 25 in the United States). It will go on to be known as the *White Album*.

1969

January 2	The Beatles begin filming *Get Back,* which will eventually be called *Let It Be.*
January 13	*Yellow Submarine,* the album, is released in the United States (January 17 in the United Kingdom).
January 30	The Beatles perform on the roof of the Apple building, their last live appearance together ever.
February 3	Allen Klein moves in to the Apple building to become the Beatles' business manager.
February 4	Eastman and Eastman becomes the Beatles' general counsel.
March 12	Paul marries Linda Eastman.
March 20	John marries Yoko Ono.
March 25	John and Yoko stage their first "bed-in" in Amsterdam.
April 11	"Get Back" / "Don't Let Me Down" is released in the United Kingdom (May 5 in the United States).
April 22	John takes Ono as his middle name; Yoko takes Lennon as her last name.
May 9	John and Yoko release *Unfinished Music No. 2—Life with the Lions* in the United Kingdom (May 26 in the United States).
May 26	John and Yoko stage their second bed-in in Montreal, Canada.

May 30	"The Ballad of John and Yoko" / "Old Brown Shoe" is released in the United Kingdom (June 4 in the United States).
June 1	John and Yoko, along with friends, record "Give Peace a Chance" from their bed in Montreal.
August 20	The Beatles are together for the last time in a studio, finishing *Abbey Road*.
August 28	Paul and Linda have a daughter, Mary.
September 26	*Abbey Road* is released in the United Kingdom (October 1 in the United States).
October 20	The Plastic Ono Band releases *Wedding Album* in the United States (November 7 in the United Kingdom).
November 25	John returns his MBE to the Queen.
December 12	The Plastic Ono Band releases *Live Peace in Toronto* worldwide.

1970

February 6	John and Yoko release "Instant Karma" / "Who Has Seen the Wind?" in the United Kingdom (February 20 in the United States).
March 6	"Let It Be" / "You Know My Name" is released in the United Kingdom (March 11 in the United States).
March 27	Ringo releases *Sentimental Journey* in the United Kingdom (April 24 in the United States).
April 10	Newspapers print Paul's quote that the Beatles won't work together again.
April 17	Paul's album *McCartney* is released in the United Kingdom (April 20 in the United States).
May 8	*Let It Be*, the album, is released in the United Kingdom (May 18 in the United States).
May 11	"The Long and Winding Road" / "For You Blue" is released in the United States.
May 13	*Let It Be*, the movie, opens in New York.

CHAPTER ONE

Liverpudlian Childhoods

Not for ourselves, but for the whole world, were we born.

Liverpool Institute motto

The Brits never saw it coming. It came in the night, soaring through the air, right above their heads. It came as destruction to everything they knew and all the values and morals they held dear. They told themselves they could clean up the damage, rebuild, that given time, the destruction could be contained, buried, and forgotten. But it was radioactive, and the fallout was reaching neighboring towns and cities at a rapid pace—the destruction was only spreading. It could not be contained, and there was no cure for it.

It was, of course, the filthy and suggestive music of none other than Elvis Presley. His existence, the Brits assumed, was limited to America, as British children were far too respectful and clean-cut to ever dabble in that nonsense. This Elvis slicked his hair back, writhed around the stage, and caused throngs of young ladies to scream, shake, or even faint, with ecstasy. When he appeared on TV, it was often only from the waist up, lest young women be led into temptation or young men led to emulate this man. British parents across the United Kingdom assumed, incorrectly, that this kind of thing could only happen in America.

But thanks to progressing technology in the 1950s, radio had become stronger, more advanced, and a common household item due to the war. When there were no more air raid warnings to be had, Belgium would transmit American music from 8 P.M. to 12 A.M. on Saturday nights, which would barely make it over the Irish Sea to the United Kingdom. And on the other side, a certain 15-year-old boy would have his ear stuck to a crotchety old radio, barely making out the songs through the fuzz and interference—but it was enough to light his soul ablaze and set his course for a destiny most would only dream of.

***

John Winston Lennon was that 15-year-old boy. He was born October 9, 1940, during a German air raid, to Julia Lennon. Julia was a free-spirited girl, who sang, played the banjo, and spoke her mind. This was most apparent when she marched up to her father, John Stanley, and announced that she had gone and married her boyfriend. Her free-spiritedness continued when her husband, Freddie Lennon, left for several years as a seaman, and she took up with another fellow. John grew up with the overwhelming feeling that he was unwanted by his own mother. "The worst pain is that of not being wanted," he once said, "of realizing your parents do not need you in the way you need them."[1] He was a sensitive child and was aware that his mother felt him as somewhat of a bother, as she enjoyed going out and being social, sometimes all night long.

Freddie returned to find Julia pregnant with another man's baby. Julia's father forced her to move out of his home, and Julia moved to Liverpool. When the baby was born—a girl—she was given up for adoption and never seen again. Freddie had offered to stand by her, but Julia had refused, and once Freddie was gone for good, she started going out night after night, meeting more and more men. This caused enough drama that Julia passed John along to her sister, Mimi Smith, to raise in a more stable environment; it was perhaps too stable for a child with his mother's rebellious streak.

Mimi lived at 251 Menlove Avenue, in a house called "Mendips," in Woolton, just outside Liverpool. Mimi was unlike Julia in nearly every way: organized, strict, and stubborn. She stepped into the role of a surrogate parent easily, picking up the slack left by Julia and taking John under her wing. While she was stubborn and authoritarian, she and John did get along, for she had a good sense of humor. She and her husband, George, loved John dearly, and John took to that environment quite well as a child, keen to have attention. The latter part of his childhood was a happy time, and he was a carefree and easygoing child and felt loved and safe. When John was 14, George passed away from a heart attack, leaving only Mimi to raise him.

John was an artistically curious young man, spending days reading Mimi's large collection of short stories, but unable to find a way to express himself. When he was 12, Mimi enrolled him in a state grammar school called Quarry Bank. Set against hordes of other young men his age, John soon realized he was different. John quickly became bored with school and anxious to pursue what he felt called to do: create. But John still didn't know what that meant or how to do it. Instead, he began rebelling.

John's best friend was another lad named Pete Shotton. Often, they would go to Liverpool to get a look at the older boys who dressed so differently and were called teddy boys. The rage in fashion was from the Edwardian period, the nickname for Edward being Ted, and hence teddy boys. Teddy boys were the first face of British youth culture after the war, and they dressed to shock the older generations, namely their parents. The dress consisted of an Edwardian-style "drape" jacket, similar to a modern sports coat, except they were longer—sometimes to the knee—with a long, narrow collar, often in velvet or a contrasting color, and single-breasted. They wore these jackets with "drainpipe" pants, which look as they sound: tight, and straight down. Their hair was equally unusual: loaded with grease, the top would cascade onto the forehead, while the sides were slicked back and combed into two flaps, like the backside of a duck, which is why the style was called a ducktail. As with most young boys, John and Pete took on the fashion of their elder youths and began trying to dress this way themselves.

Mimi was horrified with this. It was no way to dress for a boy attending Quarry Bank; however, Julia, whom John would visit frequently in Liverpool as he got older, was easygoing and even encouraged the effort by giving John money to have his trousers taken in. Along with that, John grew sideburns and slicked his hair back. By 15, John was a regular teddy boy, and he did as all the other teddy boys did: he listened to that dreadful, disgusting rock 'n' roll.

BBC radio was far too respectful to play rock 'n' roll, so John was thrilled to discover that Radio Luxembourg broadcasted this music on Saturday nights. John and Pete would drag their other teddy boy friends out to what they called "the Bank," a large grassy slope overlooking the town. The radio came through clearest there, and the summer they were turning 15, each night they could be found on the

Bank, hanging on to every beat of Elvis, Little Richard, Bill Haley, Fats Domino, and others. They weren't the only ones, either: before they had ever met, John Lennon, Paul McCartney, and Ringo Starr were all tuning in to the revolution.

***

Skiffle showed up on the music scene first, as a general compromise between unacceptable rock 'n' roll and more acceptable pop music. Skiffle was a hybrid that ran down the middle of these two genres, turning up the tempo and rhythm of pop, and turning down the scandalous lyrics of rock 'n' roll. Skiffle also had a country twang to it, as most skiffle bands used just a guitar, a bass, and an old-fashioned washboard.

Skiffle ignited the imaginations of British youth and started a fire under their feet. Skiffle was fun, but boys like John were itching to hear more and go farther. In the meantime, John attempted to satiate his thirst for music by begging both Mimi and Julia for a guitar. He eventually got one, although a variety of stories exist, and conflict, as to whether it was Mimi or Julia who purchased it. More credit lies with Julia, as she herself played the banjo, and she empathized more with John's musical curiosity than Mimi ever did. Regardless of how he got it, it showed up one day, and Mimi allowed the guitar into her home. It was a Reveille, an inexpensive guitar made by Gallotone Champion. It was quite small, made of maple wood, steel-stringed, and Spanish-looking. "Playing guitar's all very well, John," Mimi claims she said, "but you'll never make a living out of it."[2]

So John and Pete Schotton formed their first skiffle group. "Should we start a band then, Pete?"[3] asked John. When Pete mentioned that he couldn't play any instruments, John told him to take up the washboard. With that, a group was formed. Julia began teaching John banjo chords, after he got fed up with the rigid guitar lessons that came with his purchase. She taught him, and the next member of their group, a fellow schoolmate named Eric Griffiths, the chords G, C, and D7—enabling them to play a number of popular songs. So they began to practice, sometimes at Mimi's, sometimes at Julia's, and sometimes at Eric's. Without anything being said, John was the front man of the group, belting out every song and performing to no one. "He was a born performer," said Eric, "You could sense that when he sang."[4]

Secretly, Pete hated being in a band. He was dreadfully shy in front of people and loathed the idea of playing to a crowd—the band's ultimate goal, of course. So Pete recruited another boy from school, Bill Smith. Bill had a longer washboard, and by attaching a broomstick and rope to it, a bass line could be produced by pulling the rope tense and plucking away. Like the washboard, the instrument required no skill in a skiffle band—just keep the beat. Shortly after this, a boy came to school with a banjo. Rod Davis went up to Eric Griffiths and pointed out his new purchase, and Eric immediately invited him to join the band. Rod was a bit put off—he didn't know even one chord yet—but Eric assured him that skiffle required little to no real knowledge of music.

Pete's mom allowed the boys to practice in a bomb shelter in their backyard, even though she regarded John as a bad influence on her son. The first song they learned was "Rock Island Line," a skiffle hit. When they didn't know the words to a song, they just made up their own, as none of them could afford to buy records. Even though the lyrics were wrong, and every instrument was being played off key, off beat, and out of tune, when the song was over, what was left was a group of young men grinning like fools. The thrill of playing together, of making music (though the neighbors might not have called it that) was enough for them.

Now that they had a band, and a few practices under their belts, they had to choose a band name. This was no small feat for some-one like John, who understood that the name could ultimately decide their fate. They originally decided on "the Blackjacks," which sounded very American and youthful to them—but they learned that the name was taken by a more experienced band. Then Pete came up with one that stuck: at Quarry Bank school the boys were forced to stand and sing the school's anthem, "*Quarrymen, old before our birth.*" The band was born: The Quarrymen, a flippant reference to their time at school.

Soon the band picked up a drummer, Colin Hanton, whom Eric had met on the local bus. Colin could hardly play the drums, but owning a set was rare and so he was welcomed with open arms. The band also acquired a manager, a fellow student named Nigel Walley, who, due to his lack of musical ability in any form, vowed to find the band work. Nigel discovered most stores would post professional-looking posters, and suddenly all of Woolton was papered with signs offering the Quarrymen as musicians for hire.

Through April and May, the boys accepted anything they could call a gig. This mostly consisted of house parties, but nothing discouraged them. They took a few gigs at Gaumount Cinema, a local movie theater near Penny Lane, playing to kids and preteens between movies. The kids would stand on their chairs and holler at them, but the boys treated it like a serious gig nonetheless.

While the gigs were hit-and-miss, the practice was paying off. Their music was just starting to come together, and John was shining as the front man, naturally working the audience and charming the room with ease. John was greatly encouraged by the progress of the band and soon began entering them in every skiffle contest in the region. Contests were a way for venues to book gigs without paying; nevertheless, the boys went to every one they could, even if there was no money to be had. This was great practice for the boys, playing to audiences and breaking in the band.

It was late May when the *Liverpool Echo* began announcing a large talent contest. The contest was being run by Carroll Levis, a Canadian who put on amateur nights in theaters around the country. Television was not a hit in Britain yet, and few families owned a TV, so theater was still thriving. So when it was announced that Levis would put on a show in Liverpool, excitement spread quickly through the area.

It would be considered a huge production, with eight acts. The Quarrymen were nervous, playing for so many people, and plowed through their three-minute rendition of "Worried Man's Blues." After them, and the last band of the night, was the Sunnyside Skiffle Group from North Wales. Not only was the band more experienced, exciting the crowd by jumping all over the stage, they were fronted by a dwarf named Nicky Cuff, who played his bass by standing on top of it. The band had a coach and a number of supporters in the audience, and to make matters worse, they were the final band of the night. When they finished their song, the promoters realized they still had time left. So Nicky Cuff and his band were asked to play another since they were already on stage. The Quarrymen were angry, cornering Levis and insisting that this was an unfair advantage. Levis apologized but said there was nothing he could do at that point.

The winner was determined by a clap-o-meter, and most bands scored in the high 70s, except for the Quarrymen and the Sunnyside Skiffle Group. It was unusual to have a tie, but both bands received exactly 90 points in claps. The audience was asked to clap again, to determine between the two, and the Welsh group won by just a point or two. Levis apologized to the boys, saying "I might've been a bit unfair there lads, but it's too late now. Don't despair—you were quite good. Just keep at it." While it appeared dismal, there was a mighty lesson learned that night. "We got a lesson in showmanship," said Rod

Davis, "We didn't win because of the other group's antics, and that was where the germ of performing came over [us]."[5]

The boys held their heads high and pushed onward, though John was initially crushed at the loss. During this time Nigel Walley had quit school at 15 to become a professional golfer. He golfed at Lee Park, a country club founded for Jewish families that were denied membership elsewhere. One day Nigel was golfing with Dr. Joseph Sytner, and mentioned his alternate life managing the Quarrymen. Sytner's son, Alan, as it turned out, was crazy about jazz and owned two jazz clubs and was opening a third, called the Cavern. Between jazz bands, Alan would have the Swinging Bluegenes play a grown-up version of skiffle. Nigel asked if Sytner thought his son would give them a shot. Sytner said he would happily try to arrange something but wanted to hear the boys play first. This was how the Quarrymen came to play at the Lee Park Golf Club.

This was considered even more important than the Levis show, because it was an audition to play at a real club. At face value, it seemed odd that a poor teenage inexperienced skiffle group would play for a group of socially outcast Jewish folks, but the gig was too promising to pass up. The boys nearly choked when 75 people turned up for the show, but they gave it their all. With only a slight tension from the audience, the Quarrymen careened through a dozen songs from traditional skiffle to modern rock 'n' roll, and John lit up on stage more than ever, as he was singing into a real microphone—a rare occurrence. According to Nigel, John was extremely quick-witted that night, throwing out one-liners in between songs and courting the audience. The night turned out to be a huge success, especially when a hat was passed around and turned up in the boys' laps with 15 pounds in it—more than they'd ever be paid in a club. Sytner's son, Alan, contacted them that week, and they picked up that guest spot, playing between jazz bands.

Their first impression of the Cavern was that it was creepy: a tiny doorway on a deserted street that led to a dark stairway, which descended into a foul stench of mold and musk. At the bottom was a cave, essentially, with about 40 chairs and room to dance. It was hot as hell and smelled just as bad. The band took the stage for their interlude. John insisted on playing rock 'n' roll, and Rod Davis argued that it would get them tossed out of a jazz club. He launched into several rock 'n' roll numbers anyway, despite negative feedback from the audience. At some point after the third song, Alan interceded and told John to cut it out.

The gig might not have been successful, but it was a foreshadow-ing. Liverpool was in love with skiffle, but John's intuition that rock'n' roll would be the next big thing was correct. He decided that the Quarrymen would abandon skiffle and become a rock'n' roll band—a decision that made the rest of the band uncomfortable, especially Pete. Pete already felt like he never fit in—he did it just because he was John's friend; however, Pete's problems were about to be solved, as very soon John would meet his ultimate competition, a young lad with a natural talent for music of all sorts: Paul McCartney.

***

Jim McCartney was a bachelor, a humorous and romantic fellow who had never settled down; that is, until one night in June of 1940, when a German air raid caused a house party to go into lockdown, and he met eyes with a lovely lady named Mary. An unlikely pair, Jim was frisky and uncomplicated, Irish and young at heart for a 40-year-old man, while Mary was determined and strong-willed, a nurse and mid-wife, and at 31 was considered past her prime. They fell in love, and, unwilling to wait out the war, they married quickly, in April of 1941.

Then, on June 18, 1942, Mary delivered a baby boy to a team of nurses, most of them her close friends. The baby was named James, as were all first-born boys in the McCartney clan. However, Mary wasn't keen on the idea of having all these Jameses running around, so she gave him the middle name Paul—and the name stuck. Paul, and his baby brother Peter Michael (also called by his middle name), had a happy childhood roaming the hills of Speke, outside Liverpool. Paul and Mike found the vast grassy lands to be almost imaginary, from a fairytale or a far-away land, and grew up outdoors.

Jim taught the boys philosophy, while Mary read them poetry and books. Paul was very smart and took to education well, ending up qualifying for a prestigious grammar school, Liverpool Institute, which was next door to the art college John Lennon would attend. The institute's motto was *non nobis solum sed toti mundo nati*: not for ourselves, but for the whole world, were we born. Although this edu-cation was important, the main occurrence in the McCartney house was music—there was always a record playing from Jim's stash of old 78s. Jim's father, Joe, had also been musical, with a love of opera and classical styles, and this had been passed along through the genera-tions. Jim had a love of jazz, and big bands, and had learned piano as a child when his father bought one from North End Music Store, or NEMS, in 1918; Jim had even gone on to form a band, Jim Mac's Jazz Band, and performed around Liverpool through the 1920s.

As Paul became a teenager, Jim took a serious attitude toward teaching him to hear music. Jim would throw on old records and get Paul to name the instruments and chord patterns and taught him all about harmony. On his 14th birthday, Paul was presented with a trumpet, a family heirloom. This was not, however, Paul's best skill. He could make noise—but not music.

Music was not lost on him though. Paul's ear took a liking to the songs he heard on the radio, as he spent his nights tuning into Radio Luxembourg, just like John. The big bands his father enjoyed were okay, but Paul quickly developed an insatiable thirst for rock 'n' roll. Ray Charles, Fats Domino, and Little Richard rang through his ears and ripped into his little teenaged heart. He soon began begging his dad to buy him a guitar. Jim couldn't quite afford to lose nearly a month's pay to purchase a guitar, but his heart skipped at his son's interest in music. One day he wrapped up the heirloom trumpet, took it to a music store, and exchanged it. He returned home with a Zenith, a brown sunburst model. While the trumpet was worth nearly five times the guitar, Jim's sacrifice would prove pivotal to music history.

The summer of 1956 was a hot one, and it saw Paul hammering away for hours and hours every day on that guitar. A problem presented itself immediately: Paul was left-handed. He attempted to flip the guitar and play the chords upside down, as most left-handed guitarists did, but it just wasn't working. Ingeniously, Paul restrung the guitar strings and the problem was solved. Academics were forgotten quickly once Paul had the guitar to concentrate on. Discipline was never really Paul's forte, but the guitar stole his heart, and his time.

Back in 1948, Mary had started having stomach pains. They found out then that she had advanced cancer. In 1956, Mary had left the cancer unchecked and quickly began to deteriorate. She went into the hospital for a mastectomy, but it wasn't enough: the cancer had spread, and there was no hope. On October 31, 1956, Paul and Michael were shuffled into the room at the hospital to say goodbye to their mother. She lay there gaunt, wasted, and dark. The boys jumped all over her, and Mary put on a strong face for them. Jim, whose gift had always been one of optimism, stood frozen in the corner, hiding his tears from the boys. Mary passed away later that night.

Paul floated around the house, lost in the devastation of losing his mother. To distract himself, and to fill time, Paul threw himself into his guitar more than ever. Paul's grades continued to plummet, and he skipped classes more and more. His only consolation was music: rock 'n' roll was his escape, a drug that relieved him of his pain. Hours and days were spent locked away in his bedroom, listening and imaging all of it. It would take another eight months of this before Paul would learn not only to replicate his favorite songs, but also to add his own style to them. Incidentally, in eight months, he would meet John Lennon.

***

July 6, 1957, was a pleasant day. The sun was out, summer was upon them, and the Quarrymen had a gig lined up, thanks to Pete's mother, at the St. Peter's Church Fete, which usually only had marching bands. It was the biggest event of the summer in Woolton, so much so that even Paul was convinced to make the trek out from Liverpool. Paul's school friend Ivan Vaughan told him to come along and meet a lad named John. Ivan went to Dovedale elementary with John, and they had been friends ever since, even though John went on to Quarry Bank, and eventually on to Liverpool Art College, and Ivan ended up at Liverpool Institute. Ivan told Paul that John played in a cool skiffle band that he quite enjoyed, and he thought Paul would fancy meeting someone with interests similar to his own. Paul was not taken with the idea, until Ivan said the fete was a good place to meet girls.

At about 4 o'clock, the Quarrymen took the stage. Just as the party planners had hoped, the presence of the Quarrymen had brought throngs of teenagers to the event. An explosion of music came from the stage, interrupting the quaint garden party, including Mimi trying to enjoy a cup of tea. It would seem she had never realized John actually played in a band. Mimi sat with her jaw dropped, as she watched her nephew, decked out like a hoodlum, plow through a good mix of skiffle and rock 'n' roll tunes. After a raunchy rendition of "Be-Bop-A-Lula," John noticed Mimi was in the crowd, and it threw him off a bit. He spontaneously worked Mimi's name into some of the lyrics, as a cocky gesture of pride and pretension.

Both Pete and Eric noticed Ivan off to the side and were pleased. They too had grown up with Ivan, who was a charismatic and loyal friend—and even occasionally played bass with the Quarrymen. After the show, Ivan rushed up to them and introduced his friend— Paul McCartney. Ivan specifically pulled Paul over to John and forced the two to meet. Ivan told John that Paul was a great guitarist, but John was standoffish and probably threatened. John's eyes were slits as he gave Paul a once-over, Paul doing almost the same to him. Paul had brought his guitar and stole the spotlight by whipping it out and launching into "Twenty Flight Rock," by Eddie Cochran. The song had a tricky chord progression, and even John noticed the ease with which Paul played it. Also impressive was Paul's memorization of the lyrics—the correct lyrics—sung with confidence and abandon that was uncanny. Paul was a natural.

John and Paul sniffed each other out like wild dogs. Despite the threat of another alpha male, both of them seemed to sense a connection that bound them. They shared the same passion, the same love affair with music, the same commitment. One could argue it was almost love at first sight. Later John recalled "I half thought to myself, 'he's as good as me' . . . it went through my head that I'd have to keep him in line if I let him join. But he was good, so he was worth having. He also looked like Elvis. I dug him."[6]

The official exit of Pete from the Quarrymen took place at a party, where the boys were exceedingly drunk, and John crashed Pete's washboard over his head. There he sat, tears of laughter streaming down his face, his washboard hanging over his shoulders. Regardless of where and why it took place, one thing was sure: Pete Shotton was out, and Paul McCartney was in.

NOTES

1. Quoted in Bob Spitz, *The Beatles: A Biography* (New York: Time Warner Book Group, 2005), 25.
2. Quoted in Philip Norman, *John Lennon: The Life* (New York: Doubleday Canada, 2008), 58.
3. Quoted in Spitz, *The Beatles*, 49.
4. Ibid., 49.
5. Ibid., 58.
6. Quoted in Hunter Davies, *The Beatles* (New York: Norton, 1996), 33.

CHAPTER TWO

Art School Dropout

I'm going to be a rock 'n' roll singer.

John Lennon

Liverpool Art College looked like a prison from the outside, which was ironic since it was located on Hope Street. A respected art college, it served as both a prestigious art school and it sat next door to the traditional high school, Liverpool Institute, where two other would-be Beatles were attending. When John flunked out of Quarry Bank, art school was his only option aside from getting a trade, and Mimi begged Liverpool College to take him; surprisingly, they did.

John's initially indifferent attitude to school was challenged when he met Arthur Ballard, the principal, whom even John knew of by reputation—a drinker, womanizer, rebel, and former heavyweight champion. His macho attitude struck a chord in everyone—including John. Despite John's secret admiration, he played it tough; however, Mr. Ballard was similar to John in many ways—rebellious, stubborn, and cocky—and therefore he could see right through John. This, of course, made John quite uncomfortable, as he had always been able to put up a front—both on stage, and off. Luckily for John, Ballard didn't just see through him, he saw the potential inside of him, and decided to take a risk when he accepted John into the school. While Mimi rejoiced, John remained as stubborn as ever.

Summer came to an end and John geared up for another year at school by locking himself away playing guitar. He was still playing banjo chords, and he spent much of his time transposing them to guitar chords, haunted by the ease with which Paul had played at the fete. A natural leader, John was sickened by the thought of someone being better than him, and so he worked away furiously to catch up. In August, Paul contacted John to get together and play. For the very first time, John let someone else take the driver's seat and gave Paul room to teach him more about guitar. John still had to transpose the chords, as Paul played left-handed, and therefore upside-down, but John began to really see the essence of Paul. He had the whole package: he could sing on key, play with a natural ease, and give a performance all at the same time. John was raw and gritty; Paul was smooth and catchy. Although eventually it would be these differences that would drive them apart, at the time was absolutely perfect.

In September of 1957, John Lennon staggered into Liverpool College. The cafeteria was packed with an army of art students clad in neutral colors and pleasantly uninteresting attire. One of the students, Bill Harry, sat in the corner with several friends, sizing up everybody in the room, when he noticed a boy in a baby-blue Edwardian jacket, a frilly shirt, black drainpipes, with his hair duck-tailed and bushy side-burns exploding from his cheeks. "Bloody Hell!" he shouted, "that's a teddy boy there!"[1]

Bill and John immediately formed a strange, and unexpected, friendship. Bill was a classic art student, relatively soft-spoken, easily amused, and poor, while John was arrogant, outspoken, and highly cynical. Bill had to work hard to stay in school, while John literally had it forced upon him. But John was keen on Bill's off-beat sense of humor, his drawings, and the fact that he ran the school newspaper. He captured John's imagination and drew him into his group of friends almost instantly. Aside from Bill, John was also intrigued by a small, elfin-looking boy who was not only quite handsome, but a master of the paintbrush. His name was Stuart Sutcliffe, and he was one of the elite of the college, with a massive and ingenious portfolio at the age of 14. Between Bill and Stuart, John had found new sources for inspiration and settled in to the world of art school.

It would have seemed that John would have flourished under the loose rules of the school. Classes and lectures were scheduled but not mandatory. Considering his rebellion against Mimi's strict household and Quarry Bank's staunch expectations, John should have done well with the freedom to move at his own pace; in actuality, it proved to be his downfall. John resisted art, failing even the most basic courses, constantly missing class, or showing up and goofing off. In late 1957, the time came for first-years to pick their area of concentration for the rest of their time at the school. John was pulled from class and lectured—loudly—for putting out little or no effort whatsoever. John's natural response was, of course, to dig his hands deep into his pockets and grow as distant as possible. The teacher didn't give in—he yelled more, pointing out each and every one of John's shortcomings and failures. Finally John had had enough and lashed out, yelling that he never wanted to be an artist anyway. Stunned, the teacher carefully asked him what he thought he would end up doing, looking at John like he was deranged or demented. With complete conviction and unwavering confidence, John stared the teacher straight in the eyes and said "I'm going to be a rock 'n' roll singer."[2]

October 18, 1957 was the date of Paul's debut appearance with the Quarrymen, and he rehearsed relentlessly all day long. Even when the boys were out cruising the streets and catcalling at girls, Paul was in the back seat strumming away, nervously preparing for a guitar solo John was going to give him during the show. The gig was at New Clubmoor Hall, in the Norris Green part of Liverpool—considered a quite posh neighborhood. It was decided that because of the neighborhood, the boys should wear nicer clothes. The rest of the band wore white shirts with black piping, while John and Paul wore tweed sports coats. The matching coats didn't seem like much at the time, but it established that John and Paul were partners, even equals, and the front men of the band.

Halfway through the show, John stopped to introduce Paul as the latest member, and the band began playing "Guitar Boogie Shuffle" to show off Paul's fancy finger work. Paul was, for some reason, caught off guard and started a half-beat too late. He seized up and wasn't able to regain control or catch up in the song, leaving him awkwardly hammering away in the spotlight. "I blew! I just blew it!" said Paul, "... from then on, I was on rhythm guitar."[3] John seemed almost relieved that the seemingly unshakable, cocky Paul McCartney was, indeed, human after all.

Almost as surprising as John's reaction was that the promoter invited them to perform at a few other venues. The boys hastily accepted, even though the venues were in what they considered a "no-go" area:

Garston. Garston was infamously dangerous, being located near the docks, a dark area of town with a population of loitering teddy boys, sailors, seamen, and generally questionable characters. But the boys risked their lives for the sake of a shilling each and for the crowded venues. They loved playing to a full house, even if each night ended in a massive brawl in the audience, as fighting was another form of entertainment in Garston. Aside from a few private parties and dancing, the occasionally gig in Garston was about all the Quarrymen saw for the rest of the year.

When gigs slowed down, John and Paul still continued to see each other every day. They would make music, talk music, and listen to music for as much time as they could get away with. Often they could sit together, either under Mimi's criticizing eye, or while Jim McCartney was off at work, and talk for hours about the band they dreamed of creating. They shared the same hard, loose, and fast taste in music, and soon their goals and dreams were intertwined. When

Once upon a Time: John Lennon at the Woolton Fete, the day he met Paul McCartney. July 6, 1957. (AP Photo/Str.)

it came to music, something unspoken occurred between them. They understood each other. Paul looked up to John, who was older, in college, and had a tough-guy attitude; John respected Paul's talent and sought his advice on all things musical. More than that, John quickly discovered that Paul was easily corrupted, and he soon had Paul into all sorts of mischief with him, but music remained their universe. While all their idols were American—teenage stars like Gene Vincent, Buddy Holly, and Chuck Berry—the boys agreed that eventually that would change. Little did they know that they would be the very ones to usher in that revolution. First, however, they would have to collide with another up-and-coming teenage guitarist, who would give them a run for their money: George Harrison.

***

Harry Harrison was born and raised in and around Liverpool, and he instinctively followed the same footsteps as many Liverpudlians before him, including Freddie Lennon: he went to sea. The lure of faraway ports and life on a ship was about the only adventure Liverpudlians could hope for. Just before shipping out, a surprisingly confident shop girl marched right up to him and handed over her address on a slip of paper. Louise French didn't think much of it at the time—just a small burst of spontaneity that she felt posed no threat. Harry was taken, however, and though he shipped out the next day, he wrote Louise letters from African ports frequently, until she agreed to go on a real date with him. They were married a year later while Harry was on extended leave. Two children—unoriginally named Louise and Harry—and six years later, the Harrisons' small family was struggling to stay afloat on Harry's meager salary of 25 shillings a week. Harry decided to return to the mainland to be close to his family, but it was bad timing for Harry, as a depression had overtaken the motherland and the work Harry had been hoping for was scarce. The family moved to a small home in an area of South Liverpool known as Wavertree. Louise took work as a cashier, and small pockets of money came in from the government, and after two long years Harry finally found work as a busdriver. He was given the Speke–Liverpool route, and he took it very seriously. A relaxed, smiling man in private life, Harry was a rock behind the wheel. His regulars along this route found him to be an odd combination of personable, and yet distant, including, years later, frequent passenger Paul McCartney. Regardless, the job was a lifesaver, because Louise had another son, Peter, and two years after that, on February 25, 1943, she gave birth to their fourth and final child, a boy named George.

A salary less than half of what he made as a sailor left the family barely scraping by, until one day as luck would have it, the Harrisons were chosen at random from a massive waiting list of housing applicants to receive a new home from the Liverpool Corporation, for whom Harry worked. The family was given a home at 25 Upton Green, in Speke, about half a mile from where Paul McCartney lived. George fared extremely well in school at Dovedale Primary—the same elementary school John Lennon had once attended—and qualified for grammar school in no time. Harry had high hopes for his youngest son, dreaming of sending him to university and giving him the chance to do something great. George would certainly do just that, but not in the slightest in the way Harry expected.

Something changed in George upon entering the Liverpool Institute. As a young teenager, George gradually became stubborn, reckless, and rebellious to his teachers and principle. He lashed out against the school's conformity, regarding the uniforms with disdain, and instead modeled himself after the nonconformists of the era, the teddy boys. George eventually turned up at school in black drainpipes, a tight shirt, and—interestingly enough—blue suede shoes. His long hair was slicked back with handfuls of gel, rock hard and exaggerated. His only friend was another outcast and cocky boy named Arthur Kelly.

The Harrisons had always been a musical bunch. In 1932, Harry had returned home from America with a beautiful gramophone and a stack of records. Louise, although not the most talented singer, could be found around the house singing at the top of her lungs. Along with playing records during dinner, Louise and Harry would tune in to BBC every night at 8:10 P.M. to listen to the orchestra play. George would even tune in on Sundays to listen to Radio India, the hypnotizing sitars and rhythms, which no doubt left a lasting impression on him.

Much like other Liverpool boys, Arthur and George got their hands on "Rock Island Line" and that very day decided to get guitars and learn to play skiffle. George won his mother over almost instantly, and Louise gave him three pounds to buy a used guitar from a schoolmate. Arthur convinced his parents to spend the higher amount of fifteen pounds on a new model. George, however, was immensely frustrated with his inability to learn the guitar immediately, and he stashed it in a cupboard almost right away.

Then one day Arthur's brother-in-law, Red, returned home from a business trip to New York and brought with him an armful of brand new records. These were not the bulky, scratchy-sounding 78s most people were used to; they were lovely 33s and 45s with a crystal-clear sound. Arthur was most curious about the record by an oddly named bloke called Elvis Presley. Within seconds of hearing "Blue Suede Shoes," Arthur was on the phone with George. George instantly retrieved his guitar from the cupboard, after three months of hibernation.

Intoxicated by Elvis, and guitars in hand, the next step was, obviously, for Arthur and George to form a band, which they called the Rebels. The band played one gig at a local British Legion outpost, but their music didn't go over well with an audience of ex-servicemen. The Rebels began and ended in the same short season; along with his band, George abandoned skiffle and devoted himself to rock'n'roll. He began tuning in to Radio Luxembourg on Saturday night, unaware of, but alongside, John and Paul.

While chord progressions were still awkward for George, he had an unusual talent for riffs, ever since he first picked up the guitar at 13 years old. He could memorize solos after just a few plays of the record and was not only able to repeat them, and repeat them well, but add his own extra flare to them—a skill not easily come by for even the most skilled guitar players of the time. George was not interested in learning the guitar; he was obsessed with mastering it. Long, monotonous hours were spent as George worked over song after song, learning every nook and cranny, every single note. By the time he was 14, he was considered one of the best guitar players in the Liverpool Institute.

Of course, being the best took time, and like John, George's grades took a huge nosedive. He had given up on studying and focused only on music. When he even showed up at school—which was becoming rarer and rarer—he would shuffle off to the smoker's corner, where he'd loiter with about 10 other boys, smoking cigarettes and collectively mocking the conformist students, who wandered the school yard in their matching uniforms.

One of the regulars who frequented the smoker's corner was Paul. On the outside, their appearance was similar: skin-tight black drain-pipes and slicked-back hair, not to mention a shared obsession with Elvis. The only difference was that Paul quietly maintained his grades, studied hard, and spoke in a "posh" English accent, which was made more obvious next to the dirtier, grittier Scouse accent common to Liverpool. To cover it up, Paul would scatter his talk with profanities. He was accepted by the group, and by George, as an outcast, even though Paul secretly lived in both the "square" world and the "rebel" world.

Their shared interest in music brought Paul and George together, though they each had different skills. On guitar, George was expressive, while Paul was precise. It was also unusual for an upperclassman like Paul to hang out with a younger student like George, barely 14; regardless, the two formed a strong friendship and shared musical interest. Paul looked out for George in school, rode the bus with him, and felt somewhat like an older brother.

Eventually Paul mentioned to George that his band, the Quarrymen, was playing a gig down at Wilson Hall in shady Garston. The gig was set for February 6, 1958. George turned up for the show and was impressed with John and the band. A month later, on March 12, George agreed to come with Paul to meet the band, which was playing at the opening of a new skiffle club, called the Morgue. Aptly named, the venue was just two dark, dank rooms lit by one dingy light bulb, illuminating ultraviolet skeletons painted on the wall. Since the room was nearly pitch black, it took George some time to track down the boys, but he did eventually find them. Paul made the necessary introductions. Because he appeared so young, and indeed he was, John hardly noticed him at all, and the rest of the band was completely indifferent. Paul remained stubborn though, and corralled everyone into the back room for George to audition.

Without hesitating, George launched into "Guitar Boogie Shuffle," which he had learned, with impeccable detail, from an old record—the same song Paul had messed up. For the rest of the band, a song like this was completely out of their league, due to the finger work required. George, however, plowed right through it without a single hiccup. While the rest of the band was undoubtedly impressed and keen on George, John was not. John cared deeply about how the band appeared and wanted nothing to do with a rosy-cheeked fawn of a schoolboy, no matter how much gel was in his hair or how tight his pants were—no matter how talented he appeared to be.

Paul didn't give up. He arranged a "chance" meeting between the three of them on a bus. They coincidentally met up on the empty upper deck, and George, this time a bit more nervous, played a good cover of a song called "Raunchy" for John. John was still unconvinced, saying that "George was just too young . . . [he] looked even younger than Paul, and Paul looked about 10."[4] This was not the image John was going for at all. Paul argued with John, repeatedly pointing out George's undeniable talent. John did want the best for his band, and he could not deny that George was one of the best. While it meant he would have to relinquish even more of his coveted spotlight, John eventually agreed to let George in.

In the spring of 1958, three out of the four would-be Beatles were making music. This was the beginning of the end for the Quarrymen. It started with Eric Griffiths, who was deeply upset when George turned up at a rehearsal. It became apparent that John was focusing solely on skill, and Eric, while he did own a rare set of drums, had none. The next rehearsal was held hastily one day at Paul's; Eric was not informed. Eric coincidentally called Paul's house that day, only to hear the band rehearsing in the background. Rather than throw a fit, Eric walked away from the band without a fight. Enough was enough. Shortly after this, a fellow schoolmate turned band member named Len Garry, who had been playing the tea-chest bass for the group, ended up in the hospital with tubercular meningitis. He wasn't released for seven months, and by then the band had long since moved on.

***

The night Julia Lennon died changed John forever and would go on to shape most of his adult life. It was July 15, 1958, and Julia was over visiting Mimi for a cup of tea, as was normal. Nigel, the band manager, showed up looking for John; he wasn't there but he found Julia and Mimi just finishing up tea. Mimi was tired and wasn't up to walking Julia to her bus stop, as she usually did. Nigel offered to walk her, since it was night time. The two made small talk as they walked down Menlove Avenue, the street where Mimi and John lived. They hit the big junction; it was time to part ways. Julia went to cross the street to the bus stop, and Nigel carried on the other way—until he heard the screech of tires screaming to a stop and turned in time to see Julia fly through the air. She was dead on impact.

The police found John at a friend's house and escorted him to the hospital. John knew from the moment he walked in and saw the look on everyone's face that Julia was gone. Something in John fundamentally changed then—something very deep inside him broke. At school, John would sit for hours looking out the big window at the top of the main staircase. He could be found at Ye Cracke, a local pub, drinking until he could barely stand, drowning his pain. He was unstable, wavering from obnoxious to friendly to hysterical to furious, and back again, all on the turn of a dime.

When he wasn't drinking, he was hiding. Even the band hardly saw him. Everyone knew John had not just lost his mum—Julia was one of his closest friends. Although Paul had recently lost his mum too, he was of little comfort to John. Paul's mother had loved him deeply, had been there for him, and Paul could go on with his life knowing his mother had cared for him; for John, though, the sudden loss of Julia ripped open his deep wound of feeling unwanted and abandoned. This would be a wound that John would carry with him until his own death. When John began to become a recluse, Paul took over as leader of the band but could hardly persuade John to come play. John would only play alone, or with Paul. Before Mimi's death, Paul and John wrote songs at a furious pace, very quickly, sometimes working all day long; now it was impossible to get anything out of John, their once fearless leader.

The crippled Quarrymen were reduced to house parties, school dances, and social clubs once again. They played irregularly, due to the three main members being so obsessed with making music that none of them took time to find places to play it. Instead of finding gigs, they scraped together five pounds to make a demonstration album, which they hoped would impress venue managers and make them look professional. In the "studio," which was a back room of a house in Kensington owned by Percy Phillips, the boys gathered to record: John, Paul, George, Colin, and a temporary member named John Lowe. Five pounds got them a two-sided disk: The A side was a cover of the Crickets' "That'll Be the Day"; the B side was a ballad written by Paul, with help from George, called "In Spite of All Danger."

Then they lost Colin. George's dad, Harry, had got them a gig to play at the busmen's social club. While they were there, Harry informed them that the local cinema manager was there to watch them play, to maybe have them play between movies. Then Harry said the boys could go have a pint at the bar for free. One pint turned into many pints, and they boys were drunk before they retook the stage for the second half of their act. They were awful. The cinema manager left, and the man who had booked them for the show banned them. Paul was furious, mostly at John for being depressed and causing the band grief; but, still intimidated by John, Paul took it out on Colin. They had it out on the bus ride home, and Colin got off at the next stop, even though it wasn't his, and hauled his drums along with him.

When music, gigs, and booze didn't do the trick, John sought solace in girls. He'd never had a shortage—girls were drawn to his bad-boy style and hard-to-get facade (though, as most found out too late, it wasn't a facade at all). Before Julia's death, John was intimate with a particular young woman and friend of the group, Barbara Baker. She resisted John's advances for a year, afraid of getting pregnant, as contraception was only available to married women, but John had his ways and relentlessly pursued her. They were each other's first sexual experience, but John was only in it for the action, and Barb eventually left him. After Julia's death—and when John was essentially a lost soul in anguish—a young woman named Cynthia Powell caught his eye. It was odd that she did, for though she was lovely, she was quiet, gentle, and polite—a far cry from his outgoing, wild mother and strong, diligent aunt. Cynthia was neat, careful, and studious, and from a posh town called Hoylake.

Cynthia took notice of John first. She longed for lettering class, where John would sit behind her and tease her mercilessly for her orderly brushes, often knocking them off the table or trying to mess up her print. She was jealous of other girls who got close to John, and she made changes accordingly. She grew out her perfect perm into longer, mousy locks, and dyed her hair blond. She traded in her modest outfits for a more teddy girl style. At a school dance, John, egged on by his friends, shyly asked Cynthia to dance. Cynthia had had a few drinks and was light-headed, and having John so close made her so nervous she felt sick. As they danced, John asked her if she fancied going for a drink. She was so thrown off that she hastily replied, "I'm engaged!" John snorted at the remark, shooting back, "I didn't ask you to marry me, did I?"[5] Cynthia thought she had blown it, but later that night John and his friends asked her to join them for a drink. This time she went; in fact, only hours later, they snuck away from the pub and went to Stuart Sutcliffe's flat, where they slept together.

Surprisingly, the two of them continued to see each other. In autumn of 1958, Cynthia called off her engagement back home to go steady with John. Everyone was surprised by this strange, mismatched couple. Most of Cynthia's friends warned her not to continue with John, but she was taken with him. John too, was very taken with Cynthia—she seemed to tame his anger, curb his pain; Cynthia calmed him. To keep his attention, Cynthia began showing up in fishnet stockings, garter belts, and short skirts—though she was never quite comfortable with looking so sexual. In return, John protected her with his furious temper against anyone who so much as looked at her. John demanded her complete and total obedience to him; Cynthia, mercilessly in love, complied.

The year 1959 rolled around, and rock 'n' roll started to gain favor among youth. Rock 'n' roll songs were climbing the charts, and youth everywhere were intoxicated by them. Cliff Richard emerged as the United Kingdom's answer to rock 'n' roll, along the lines of Buddy Holly and Elvis. British teens squealed for him, but anyone with a real taste for music could see he was too mainstream, too safe. Yet Cliff Richard still blazed a trail for other bands, because anyone paying attention saw the potential of this new trend; new rock 'n' roll venues opened everywhere, from pubs to schools to empty churches. The Quarrymen now had competition, and, just as John had predicted, skiffle bands were being reborn as rock 'n' roll, and every teenage boy in the city picked up a guitar, thinking he was the next Elvis. The Quarrymen had more experience though, a leading edge—but they still had a long way to go.

NOTES

1. Quoted in Bob Spitz, *The Beatles: A Biography* (New York: Time Warner Book Group, 2005), 103.
2. Ibid, 108.
3. Quoted in Keith Badman, *The Beatles: Off the Record* (New York: Music Sales Corp, 2000), 17.
4. Quoted in Hunter Davies, *The Beatles* (New York: Norton, 1996), 44–45.
5. Quoted in Cynthia Lennon, *John* (New York: Random House, 2005), 28–30.

CHAPTER THREE

Rockin' the Casbah

They're going to be the greatest, and I want to be a part of it.
Stu Sutcliffe

During the time John Lennon was so depressed, the others had to find different ways to fill their time. Paul focused on school, while George took up with another band, called the Les Stewart Quartet. A fellow band member named Ken Brown, who had also played occasionally with the Quarrymen, suggested that their band go see if they could get a gig in a new venue opening up in Liverpool. With no gigs for the Quarrymen on the docket, George was game.

It was called the Casbah. It was the brainchild of Mrs. Mona Best, when her son Pete mentioned that their massive unfurnished cellar, in their home at 8 Hayman's Green, would make a great nightclub. Mona, trapped in a bad marriage, jumped at the idea of a project to distract her. They worked away preparing to open their home to the public on August 29, 1959. Ken Brown presented himself at the Best home and offered to help get everything ready; in exchange, Mona agreed that his band could play opening night. But as August 29 rolled around, Brown got into a argument with Les Stewart, the front man of their band, and Les refused to play. Mona, worried that she would have no band for her opening night, asked George if he knew anyone else that could play. As it turns out, George did, and the Quarrymen filled in.

The opening night was a big hit. The Casbah was a packed house of wide-eyed kids, enthralled by the atmosphere: smoky, loud, and chaotic. It was here, in the Casbah, that youth came to be youth, to dance and yell and leave behind their social status, their jobs, and their predestined lives in Liverpool. Leaving behind the outside world, teenagers would lose themselves, and find themselves, amidst the mayhem of the Bests' basement. It was here that John, Paul, and George got a taste of fame, alongside Ken Brown. It was here that Paul met Dot, a frail, sharp young lady who, with an alcoholic father, shared his ache of a missing parent. Soon enough, Paul and Dot were an item, and Dot joined Cynthia at the sidelines each and every Saturday night at the Casbah.

The Quarrymen had become a roaring success, with as many as 1,300 teenagers passing through the Best home on any given night, packing their basement with as many as 400 kids at a time. The Quarrymen filled the house every weekend for seven weeks, and it all seemed too good to be true—until it fell apart because of £0.75. That seventh week, Ken turned up sick and crashed upstairs on Mona's couch. The other three went on without him, playing to yet another full house. At the end of the evening, Mona paid Ken his quarter of the band's £3 pay. John, Paul, and George flew into a rage over it: they had done the work, they deserved the money. Mona didn't budge, and the Quarrymen didn't play the Casbah again.

Without the Casbah the band's popularity took a formidable hit, but there were other opportunities to be had. The band had another shot at a Carroll Levis's show—this time for television. Every band in Liverpool appeared for the audition, and the Quarrymen made it through to the second round, to be held in Manchester, the winner of which would go on to appear on the show. When they went, they showed up with a new name: Johnny and the Moondogs. Though the band played very well that night, the final judging for the acts—the part based on the audience cheers—was not scheduled to take place until very late in the night, well after the last bus had left. With an eye on the clock and no money to stay in a hotel, the boys headed home reluctantly, and with broken hearts—although not before John slyly stole his first electric guitar, which another band had left unattended.

John knew the band could not be considered rock 'n' roll if it didn't have a bass and drums. So when his friend Stuart Sutcliffe, also known as Stu, sold a piece of art at a highly acclaimed exhibition for £65, John offhandedly suggested Stu buy a bass guitar. Once only acquaintances, Stu and John had become essentially best friends. John was near to being tossed out of Liverpool College, but Principal Ballard intervened on his behalf and John got a second chance—so long as John worked on an area of concentration. Mr. Ballard enlisted Stu to help John focus. It worked: Stu had a way of working with John that helped him let his guard down and, for once, learn. The two of them would stay late after school and Stu would show John how to experiment with painting—to throw the paint, mix it with different oils, use sand for texture, and try a plethora of other ideas. John was captivated by Stu, by his art and his ability to express himself— something John was still struggling to do. In return, John educated Stu about music, hauling records along and playing rock 'n' roll while they painted. John practically moved in with Stu, especially when Stu got a big apartment with an extra room that doubled as a rehearsal spot. Stu got John to read books; John got Stu to listen to music. Stu had the same rush of adrenaline in front of a canvas as John did in front of a crowd—and this bonded them together. So when John suggested Stu play the bass, Stu was not against the idea. His other friends questioned him for giving up art, to which Stu replied "They're going to be the greatest. And I want to be a part of it."[1]

When Stu joined the group near the end of 1959, it seemed the time had come to settle on a more mature band name. The Quarrymen had too many ties with the school, giving people the impression they were young, and perhaps inexperienced; Johnny and the Moondogs seemed too silly to them. John was pondering Buddy Holly's band, the Crickets, when the idea of *beetles* came into his head.[2] Then John suggested they spell it *beat*, as in a musical beat, and thus the name the Beatals was born, though it would need to be respelled two more times before sticking.

Of course the addition of Stu and the name change did not launch them into stardom; there was still a long road ahead. Mainly, they had no drummer—and therefore could not be considered much of a real band, not to mention that Stu hardly knew how to handle a bass guitar—though he did have the right look that made girls swoon with his delicate face, arty style, and massive bass slung over his shoulder. John worked with Stu nightly to help him learn music, while the band searched high and low for anyone that could keep a rhythm.

During these searches the boys realized that the next big step, after teaching their bass player to play, and finding a drummer, was making a big sound—literally. Real bands had amplifiers, and real rock 'n' roll was meant to be loud, almost by definition. Since everyone was poor as dirt, and amplifiers were a mighty cost, John devised quite an intelligent plan. Stu was a member of the school's Student Union committee, along with their friend Bill Harry. Both Stu and Bill proposed, and seconded, a motion to purchase sound equipment for the college's dances. No one opposed. Suddenly, and with no money from their own pockets, the Beatals had access to state-of-the-art amplification. There was a dance that very month, and the Beatals packed the basement with rowdy art students and big sound.

Aside from using the school's sound system for rocking parties, the band spent most of their days in their local hangout, the Jacaranda. The Jac, as they called it, had always been pretty popular. It had opened in 1958 by two hipsters, Allan Williams and his wife Beryl, who had spent their youth hitchhiking across Europe and hanging out in cafes. The Jac appealed to art students, jazz fans, and bohemians alike. That's where John and Stu would sit, sometimes all day, to talk art, music, and philosophy.

The Jac also had a tiny cellar, just small enough to stuff a band in and a few people to listen. The first band Beryl and Allan brought in was the Royal Caribbean Steel Band, lead by a Trinidadian man named Harold Phillips. Although the steel band proved to be popular, Allan Williams was slowly realizing that the demand for rock 'n' roll could provide a good cash flow, as he was watching teenagers go wild at an Eddie Cochran and Gene Vincent concert. He foresaw his next venture: first it was arty cafes; now it was going to be rock 'n' roll concerts. His first move was traveling to London to meet with an infamous man named Larry Parnes.

Larry Parnes had the monopoly on British musical acts, and a good eye for the next big thing. For Larry, a flamboyantly gay man, the next big thing was always another handsome young man. He would find cute teenage boys and single-handedly mold them into overnight sensations and teen idols, with a catchy name to boot. Larry was only 24 years old but had an impressive resume of these everyday-boys-turned-stars: Billy Fury, Tommy Steele, Johnny Gentle, Dickie Pride, Vince Eager, and Marty Wilde, to name a few.

Allan approached Larry about having some of his teen idols headline a concert, supported by local Liverpool bands. Larry dug the idea and agreed, and for a £500 fee, the two hashed out a plan they called "The Merseyside and International Beat Show." Larry booked Gene Vincent and Eddie Cochran, along with a dozen or so of his other teen sensations, backed by local bands Cass and the Cassanovas, and Rory Storm and the Hurricanes. Booked for May 3, 1960, all the signs told Allan that this would be a huge hit.

A huge hit was right—but not the kind Allan expected. On April 17, 1960, barely three weeks before the big show, Eddie Cochran and Gene Vincent were in a terrible car accident when their van blew a tire. Eddie died on the spot, and Gene was rushed to the hospital. Weeks passed while Allan waited to hear if Gene would still play the show, worried everything was falling through. Gene agreed to play, though there was still the massive problem of losing Eddie. Lacking another major headliner, Larry added two other groups, Julian X and Dean Webb. Allan, attempting to fill the gap, added half a dozen more local groups—but not the Beatals, who still didn't have a drummer. The boys were regulars at the Jac, though, so Allan got them stageside tickets to the show to make up for not asking them to play. The boys were heartbroken not to be on stage and ragingly jealous of the bands who got to play, for example the Hurricanes, who had talented drummers like Ritchie Starkey, affectionately known as "Ringo." It was the kick in the behind that they needed to find a real drummer.

The concert was still a major hit, even though it had lost a major headlining band. Local musicians stole the show, and the music scene in Liverpool exploded. So did the Jac—nearly every hour of every day the Jac was full of musicians talking music. The Beatals were on the outskirts then, overshadowed by "real" bands and seen as young and immature. Brian Casser, of Cass and the Cassanovas, was the first one to give them a shot. He had overheard them practicing in the basement and invited John into his inner circle. There Brian, referred to as Cass, spoke with John about the necessity of finding a drummer and also convinced John that a band must focus on its leader. Like many other bands—Cass and the Cassanovas, Buddy Holly and the Crickets, Gerry and the Pacemakers—Cass told John he needed to be the forefront of the band's name. Cass came up with Long John and the Silver Beetles. John was not impressed by the play on "Long John Silver"—a pirate—but to satisfy him, and in hopes that Cass would find them a drummer, John struck a compromise and the band name changed once again: The Silver Beetles.

Cass came through and delivered the boys a drummer: Tommy Moore. While they were excited to have a drummer again, they were stunned by Tommy: first, he was a professional drummer; and second, he was almost twice their age. Tommy was experienced and could play just about anything, but he just didn't know rock 'n' roll. His drumming was very clean, something one might hear in a lounge or a nice restaurant. Still—a drummer was at their door and they happily let him in.

While this was happening, Larry Parnes contacted Allan and congratulated him on a great show. Larry was impressed with the Liverpool bands and was considering some kind of tour. This would require Allan to represent the local bands. If it had been a cartoon, a light bulb would have lit up over Allan's head, and dollar signs would have appeared in his eyes. Of course he should represent these bands; they practically lived at his cafe, and he knew nearly all of them by name. Jacaranda Enterprises was born.

Just one day after the Silver Beetles had found their drummer, Allan got a letter from Larry Parnes, stating that Duffy Power and Johnny Gentle were looking for opening acts to play with them on their upcoming Scottish tour. Already Allan had signed on a plethora of bands to Jacaranda Enterprises, including Cass and the Cassanovas. Allan approached Cass about any other bands he should consider for the tour, and Cass told him: the Silver Beetles. With that, the group had their first major audition on May 10, 1960.

The audition was held at another club Allan had recently purchased, the Wyvern Social Club. The Silver Beetles arrived at 11 A.M., except for Tommy Moore, who was getting his drums from another club and would be on his way shortly. The other bands had already arrived, dressed in their best suits, while the Silver Beetles showed up looking like a gang in all black. Larry Parnes arrived with Billy Fury, an unexpected guest of honor, who had recently decided that he too needed backing groups for his tour. His presence overwhelmed the bands, even the stubborn and prideful John Lennon, who humbly requested an autograph.

The Cassanovas played first, followed by Derry and the Seniors, then Gerry and the Pacemakers, and finally Cliff Roberts and the Rockers. It seemed each band was wracked with nervousness by Billy Fury's unexpected presence, but the Silver Beetles remained cool and collected, as they knew they had nothing to lose. However, when their turn came they found there was one glitch: Tommy Moore was nowhere to be found. John asked the drummer from the Cassanovas to sub for them—he agreed, which was surprising since the bands were essentially competing. Even with a drummer that they'd never played with, the Silver Beetles blew everybody away. John and Paul sang together effortlessly, back and forth on the vocals as if they could read each other's minds. With their all-black attire, and rock 'n' roll attitude, the Silver Beetles stood out like stars from the other bands. Almost immediately, Billy Fury gave Larry the signal that this was the band he wanted. Then Tommy Moore came staggering through the door and took over the drums. Suddenly, the music lost all its catchiness, angst, and power. It was obvious that Tommy Moore was not the right drummer for them.

Allan and Larry went to the Jac to work out details. The bands followed them and huddled outside the door to await their decision. Larry abruptly decided that Billy Fury didn't need a backing band, so neither the Silver Beetles nor the Cassanovas would get the spot. It was then decided that the Cassanovas would open for Duffy Power, and the Silver Beetles would open for Johnny Gentle, on the Scottish tours. For the Cassanovas, it was a bit of a letdown, but for the Silver Beetles, it was unbearably exciting: all five of them, on tour, getting paid.

***

People of all types scrambled to catch their morning train on the fogged-in platform. Businessmen, conductors, tourists, laborers, and commuters pushed this way and that as they rushed to get aboard. On this day, May 20, 1960, in the middle of the chaos, sat four teenagers and an older man: John, Paul, George, Stu, and Tommy. Flanked by their meager luggage, they sat, bewildered by the commotion. Soon, they shoved their way to the train bound for Glasgow and left Liverpool behind.

It took 10 hours to get to Glasgow. From there they had to switch to another train, on the local line, to make their way up the coast. They arrived in Alloa, Scotland, in the late afternoon. Alloa was home to 14,000 Scots, most of whom had honest jobs in whiskey distilleries or as fishermen. Despite the seemingly quiet towns, there was a solid concert circuit to be had: teenaged Scots would come from all over for a good show. Usually it featured the latest sensation, such as one of Larry Parnes's boys, and several hundred kids would show up, ready to let loose.

The boys arrived late and went straight to the venue. Johnny Gentle was waiting for them, and the bands got to work. The Silver Beetles had taken time to learn most of Johnny's songs, but there was still a performance to work on, and songs to pick. The first night went well: the crowd enjoyed the mix of rock 'n' roll and sleepy ballads, and both Johnny Gentle and the Silver Beetles delivered good sets.

The bands got into a good rhythm: Johnny entertained and brought his name with him, and the Silver Beetles got things wild and rowdy. While girls fawned over Johnny and it was his name that sold tickets, the Silver Beetles would wail away on their guitars, playing as loud and fast as they could, kicking the Scots all up into a fury of yelling, singing, movement, and sweat. Quickly the boys realized, much to their delight, that while girls showed up for Johnny, they stayed for the Silver Beetles.

Nights were long as the band brought girls back to their "hotel" or whatever meager living conditions they had—often all of them in one room—taking turns or just getting down to business in the hallways or staircases. They quickly realized that rock 'n' roll music wasn't only about music—it was just as much, if not more so, about sex. After being up all night long, they'd drag themselves out of bed to carry on, pack up, and step over sleeping teenage girls strewn across the floor on their way out.

One particular morning as they packed up, Johnny decided to drive the van. John was sleeping in the front seat, and the rest of the boys slept in the back, having been up with girls until 6 A.M. Johnny got confused at a crossroad and slammed into another car. He jumped out to make sure the couple in the other car was okay, but the woman told him he should take care of his friend instead. When Johnny turned around, he saw Tommy, who had been in the backseat, on top of John in the front seat, covered in blood. Tommy was okay, but he'd lost a tooth and nearly knocked out a few others. At the hospital, he asked John if he could get out of playing that night, and John's temper flared. He demanded Tommy get out of bed and get to the show, leaning over Tommy threateningly. Needless to say, the show went on.

Car crashes weren't the only way the boys were in danger: as it turns out, Scottish males did not much enjoy their girlfriends swooning over a bunch of Scousers. The Silver Beetles didn't do much to deter them either, since they loved the attention and the action. So nearly each night they took the stage, made eyes at girls, played louder and harder as the girls drew nearer, and made sure to dodge the flying beer bottles and ashtrays incoming from the aforementioned males. Bruises and cuts abounded when the ashtrays struck their target, but even worse damage took place after the show when fists flew instead of bottles, as they were always outnumbered. Broken ribs, black eyes, swollen cheeks, bloody noses, and loose teeth were common. To add insult to injury, they were underfed, under-rested, and overworked. They simply could not defend themselves. Despite physical threats to their well-being, they accepted the risks—and the girls.

Then, suddenly, they found themselves once again without a drummer. Tommy, 15 years their senior, threw in the towel one night without so much as a Dear John. The truth was that he was hardly speaking to any of them by the end of the tour, but the young musicians were so self-involved and distracted by the thralls of touring they barely noticed, or cared. When the band returned to Liverpool, Tommy left and went back to his factory job. The others were crushed to be back at square one, after thinking they had finally made it as a band.

It was around this time that the band made its final name change, one they would stick with. A visiting poet of rising fame, Royston Ellis, came to read his beat poetry at some venues around Liverpool, including the Cavern. He was at the Jac when he was chatted up by a little fellow named George Harrison. George convinced Royston to let his band play behind him as he read poetry down in the Cavern. After the show, Royston, then only 19, told them to abandon school and work, and go for their dreams, as he had done years earlier. He then said that they shouldn't be called the Beatals, or the Silver Beetles, but a combination of the two, which would make the name easier to read but still be a pun on beat music: the Beatles. The boys, with stars in their eyes, agreed, heeding any and all of Royston's advice. Finally, the Beatles had their name, never dreaming of how famous the name would come to be.[3]

Meanwhile, Allan Williams was thinking up new tours on which to send his recently signed bands. He remembered that a few years ago, he and his wife Beryl had picked up a young German hitchhiker named Rudiger, who regaled them with tales of a city called Hamburg. Hamburg was the Amsterdam of Germany: full of sex, drugs, and gambling. It was a town where one could find any illicit thing he or she desired. As a port town, the city reached out to sailors and shipmen, who, after long months at sea, were looking for a good time.

Since World War II was less than two decades prior at the time, there were many British and American soldiers, and other expatriates, living in Hamburg. With them they brought the demand for entertainment—and not just more strippers. They wanted live music and introduced this form of entertainment to the local Germans, as well as travelers from neighboring countries. Hamburg became a hub for live music, especially American-style rock 'n' roll.

Allan booked a trip to Hamburg to check it out, sometime in July of 1960. He wandered up and down the red-light district of the city, poking his head into strip clubs, bars, and pubs. He came across a place called the Kaiserkeller, a seemingly dark and dreary bar. But when he stopped and listened, what he heard was pure gold. Well, it was actually the opposite: it was an awful German band trying to sing American songs, but they didn't speak a bit of English. This was gold to Allan because he saw an opportunity to bring English bands over to perform covers of American songs. He strolled into the Kaiserkeller and asked to speak with the owner, who, he learned, was named Bruno Koschmider. Bruno, wearing a ludicrous wig, came over to hear Allan out. Allan claimed he was a manager of famous British bands, amazing bands that would blow Hamburg away. Allan demanded £100 a week—a ridiculous sum—and Bruno nearly agreed. Allan handed him a tape, ready to close the deal, but the tape turned out to be broken and the music came out garbled. Tucking his tail between his legs, Allan bid Bruno adieu and shyly left the bar.

Allan thought he'd blown his chance, but luckily he was wrong. After he returned to Britain he got to work on shopping around his best bands. That same July he took Derry and the Seniors into London to audition at the infamous Two I's coffee bar in Soho. Allan knew the owner and had convinced him to take a listen. As the Seniors got ready, Allan jumped when he noticed a man with a bad wig: Bruno Koschmider! Bruno leapt with similar excitement to see Allan, though the men barely knew each other. As it turned out, Allan had really interested Bruno in the idea of bringing British bands to play in Hamburg, so Bruno had come to take a look. He liked the look of the Seniors and made Allan an offer on the spot. Allan, and the band, hastily accepted.

The Seniors were a hit. Hamburg loved them and they loved playing for Hamburg. Living in a sad excuse for a basement with no shower was unpleasant, but they got all the free vodka they could handle, so they were happy. Playing nearly four hours a night, the band was exhausted. They were also shocked by how upfront German girls were, by how forward and openly sexual they were; they were also shocked when they all got gonorrhea. Girls and booze abounded, and showers and beds were lacking, but the Seniors were happy as could be. Eventually, Koschmider demanded another band, and Allan sent word that one was on their way: the Beatles.

Of course, the Beatles were not Allan's first choice. He had a plethora of good local talent in his brood, and he originally offered the gig to Rory Storm and the Hurricanes, but they were on a contract in Wales until the fall. Then he tried Gerry and the Pacemakers, but they felt it was senseless to quit their jobs for short-term work.

Stu approached Allan, saying that his band was ready, and Allan reluctantly agreed, so long as the boys got a drummer.

As luck would have it, they wandered into the Casbah one night, having not been back as a group since they walked out over a few pounds six months earlier. The Blackjacks were playing, and lo and behold, Pete Best, Mona's son, was on drums. Not only was his drum kit brand new, but he was actually good at playing it—with a real understanding of rock 'n' roll, not just mechanical like Tommy. Pete agreed to join them in Hamburg, forsaking teaching college to pursue music. On August 16, 1960, they left for Hamburg, Germany.

NOTES

1. Quoted in Bob Spitz, *The Beatles: A Biography* (New York: Time Warner Book Group, 2005), 174.
2. Hunter Davies, *The Beatles,* 2nd rev. ed. (New York: Norton, 1996), 64.
3. Philip Norman, *John Lennon: The Life* (New York: Doubleday Canada, 2008), 186.

CHAPTER FOUR

An Apprenticeship on the Reeperbahn

Mach Schau!

Bruno Koschmider

Hamburg itself was not all bad, similar to Liverpool in many ways, foggy and gray, bleak and working class, but the district the band was headed to, St. Pauli, was a whole other story. When they swung around the bend that began the St. Pauli district, to a long strip of streets called the Reeperbahn, all their jaws dropped. Neon lights flashing images of nude girls illuminated the shaggy, unkempt streets, as bars, clubs, and cafes stood neck-and-neck, lining every inch of the block. Hot pink, electric blue, and fluorescent green signs blinked on and off in a scattered rhythm, all of them calling out to passers-by: "Open! Open! Open!" no matter what time of day.

Allan pulled up in front of the Kaiserkeller and proudly showed the group their new home. As they strolled inside, their eyes twinkled with delight, and they stood in awe of the sheer size of the venue. It was bigger and better and brighter than they could have imagined. The bar was shaped like a boat, the ceiling covered in fishing nets, and real brass figures that had been saved from the docks hung around the room. Bruno appeared and introduced himself, and then he quickly crushed their dreams when he escorted them to where they were actually meant to play: the Indra.

The Indra didn't hold a candle to the Kaiserkeller. It was dark, depressing, and grossly underpopulated by patrons. The group sulked, despite Bruno's assurance to them of his plans to make the Indra the next Kaiserkeller. On top of their big letdown, they were vastly unprepared for the crowds in Hamburg. Back home, they had powered through an hour or so of music to a bunch of teenagers; here, they were required to play an incomprehensible four and a half hours a night, to a bunch of sailors and drunks. Making sure they had enough songs proved to be the lesser problem at the Indra. The real problem was showmanship. Upset by the sad state of the Indra, especially in comparison to the Kaiserkeller, unimpressed by the small crowds, and exhausted from the long trip to Germany, they simply stopped trying.

Quite soon after their arrival, Bruno walked into the Indra to find them playing a barely audible version of a rock song. He marched up to the stage and laid it on the line that they would be out of there fast if they couldn't "mach schau," or "make a show." This pushed John over the edge—they were musicians, not trained monkeys. John started jumping around the stage, impersonating and mocking other bands that "made a show." But the audience, and Bruno, were serious, chanting "Mach Schau! Mach Schau!" This got the band going—all of them started jumping around, wheeling their arms and legs, and throwing their instruments around.[1]

Considering they were just joking, the crowd loved it. Bruno was right—they needed to learn how to be showmen, even if they felt like animals in a zoo. A corner had been turned, and suddenly the Beatles were the next big thing on the Reeperbahn. Within weeks the Indra was jammed every night as word spread about the new band from England. They got a break after each 45-minute set, but it was barely time to have a beer or use a bathroom. John and the band would play for up to five hours, and well into the night, past 2 A.M. Then, due to the wild ruckus they had caused, they would be too awake to sleep until a few hours later, sometimes not until it was already morning. Not that they would really want to sleep in their rooms: their accommodation was a storage locker in the back of a cinema, a few freezing and dirty rooms with some couches and no light.

Despite the long working hours, the drinking that inevitably occurred every night (Bruno paid them with small wages and free beer), the lack of food (overpriced in such a touristy neighborhood), and the awful sleeping conditions, they still found time to practice. They would meet in the afternoons to rehearse, but soon they had forsaken learning new songs and instead chose to draw out the ones they already knew. A song was usually two or three minutes, and they needed to play for five hours, so it just made sense to kill time by making the songs longer. Soon songs began to last 15 or 20 minutes if they kept at it—and so long as they kept it loud and wild the crowd was none the wiser.

Then a few things changed very quickly. First, the suits they had brought were ripped to shreds and smelled awful from all the long nights on stage (in fact, they'd been ruined within the first week). They were introduced to the Texas Shop, where they found black leather jackets and jeans, which gave them an entirely new look; little did they know they were starting a brand new trend. Next, noise complaints, of all things, were coming from nearby neighbors. Given the Indra's position on the street, the bar was within earshot of the first block of residential homes. The cops started coming around, telling Bruno to turn the music down—a ludicrous request for such a place. It so happened that Derry and the Seniors, over at the Kaiserkeller—which received no noise complaints—had only one week left on their contract. In one quick decision, Bruno closed the Indra and moved the Beatles over to the Kaiserkeller. Suddenly they had a new look, and a new stage: things appeared to be looking up.

The Seniors finished their contract on October 5, and Bruno contacted Allan to send another band. Allan immediately sent over Rory Storm and the Hurricanes. At first, the Beatles were not very impressed with the Hurricanes, who lacked stage presence and had average musical talent. Even their lead man, Rory Storm, didn't really have what it took to take the lead spot, nor did the band really know how to follow him. In fact, the only person who had much talent at all was that drummer they had been so envious of at Allan Williams's concert, Ringo.

The bands played well together though, with long rollicking jams and crazier antics as they tried to top each other. They would throw themselves around the stage, playing louder and louder on each song, and swear into the microphone in English, mocking the crowd. Once, George performed with a toilet seat over his head; another time Paul performed in a bed sheet; still another time, John mooned the audience. Because of this, the Germans started referring to the Beatles as *verruckt*: crazy. Of course, the crowds on the Reeperbahn loved all things crazy, and therefore the Beatles' popularity picked up speed. To keep them *verruckt*, patrons would send beer up to the stage, which they had to chug. Sometimes they sent hard liquor, like shots of schnapps. Sometimes they sent pills.

It was the pills that started doing real damage to the Beatles. Playing until the wee hours of the morning, rarely sleeping, eating awful food, and drinking copious amounts of beer took a toll on their energy levels and their health, and these pills didn't help. The pills sent up to them were amphetamines, or speed. Once they realized speed could keep them going, they were almost instantly hooked. They could stay awake for days at a time, if necessary; and it sometimes was. John, already en route to being an alcoholic, ate pills like candy, with George close behind. Paul and Stu dabbled, to a lesser degree, but also came to rely on the pills to keep going. Only Pete Best was able to avoid the pills all together.

While a lot of patrons returned again and again, one particular group began catching the bands' attention. Two men and a woman would come in every single night at 9 p.m. for the show. Dressed far too extravagantly for a place like the Kaiserkeller, they stood out among the crowd in their suede jackets and wool sweaters. Stu took an immediate interest in them, as all three of the mystery fans were very good looking and eluded a mysterious presence. Once introduced, he learned they were German locals, and former art students, which may have been why Stu felt such a pull to them. The two men were Klaus Voorman and Jurgen Vollmer, incredibly handsome and confident. The woman was Astrid Kirchherr, a knockout with her blond hair and icy blue eyes. Stu immediately fell in love with Astrid. Astrid claimed that she too fell in love with Stu, just moments after meeting him, and the two began a mutual infatuation. Astrid and Klaus were in a relationship at the time, but soon enough, he was ousted by Stu. Surprisingly, Klaus did not hold a grudge; he even continued hanging out with them as a group. He simply stepped aside like a gentleman and let it be.

Klaus, Jurgen, and Astrid had already pegged Stu as a fellow artist—as he was dark, moody and sophisticated—and took a great liking to him. As the four of them became friends, and as Stu and Astrid were beginning their love affair, Astrid was also working her way into the rest of the band. She did this through her camera, offering to take photos of the band for free. The Beatles jumped at this offer instantly. The photographs taken by Astrid are among the first of the band together. Unlike most other bands' photos, usually of the band lined up neatly and well-presented, these photos were dark and edgy, like Astrid; moreover, Astrid's technique of shadowing half the face was ahead of her time. The photos would become iconic in the years to come, capturing the essence of a rock band with their eerie and artistic form, and the shadow technique was duplicated time and time again.

During this time a new club opened up called the Top Ten, on October 21, 1960. An infamous singer named Tony Sheridan was headlining, and the new club was huge, and well-maintained. The Beatles went to see Tony play all the time, as he had great show-manship and worked an audience well. They got ideas for new songs from listening to his sets, and new tricks to give their own act some oomph. Soon, both the Beatles and Rory Storm were jumping on stage to play with Tony, even though they weren't getting paid. It be-came obvious to everyone that the Top Ten was a better venue, and the Beatles made plans to somehow get in there. They approached the owner of the Top Ten, Peter Eckhorn, who recognized them and saw an opportunity at hand. He offered them the gig right there. Bruno Koschmider was outraged to be undermined by his own group and terminated their contract.

During all this, someone tipped off the police that little George Harrison was only 17, and therefore underage. Unfortunately, there was a curfew in effect in Hamburg: anyone younger than 18 had to be at home by 10 P.M. George had avoided it by always being on stage when the police came around to check IDs, but one night the po-lice came and specifically checked George. Upon finding out he was under 18, they also found out he didn't have a proper work permit. George was sent back to England within 24 hours.

Meanwhile, Peter Eckhorn had offered the remaining Beatles a nice apartment above the Top Ten. Eager to get out of the hole they had been living in, they quickly and quietly packed up all their be-longings. With no light in their cave of a room, they nailed con-doms to the stone walls and lit them on fire, making very tiny flames, enough to grab their stuff and go. When Koschmider realized they were gone, he was furious; he also noticed the small burn marks on the walls. The Beatles awoke in their new apartment to police pounding at the door, with a report that claimed they had tried to burn down the Kaiserkeller.[2] Paul and Pete were deported together. John went home by train. Stu got sick and went to stay with Astrid. The Beat-les returned to England disgraced, and broke. They could hardly face their families, let alone each other. It seemed as though the adventure was over.

***

Cynthia Powell and Dot Rhone had patiently awaited the return of John and Paul, who had written them religiously while away, and in blissful ignorance, the young women cast aside what they knew of Hamburg, and embraced their beloveds upon return. They had sworn their fidelity, and the girls refused to question it. Of course, both John and Paul had had many women during their travels, sometimes a few at a time, and definitely more than they could count. For example, when returning to their tiny dark rooms after a show, anonymous girls would be waiting in their beds and, more often than not, they would never even see the girl they were in bed with. As well, Hamburg abounded with transvestites, orgies, sodomy, and more nudity than any young man could hope for, and they probably learned more about sex in those few months than any regular Liverpudlian would in a lifetime. Still, they were happy to be back in the arms of their faithful girlfriends, despite returning home with their tails between their legs.

For weeks, no one in the band spoke. They had shamed themselves, having bragged to everyone in Liverpool about the money and fame that awaited them in Germany. Now, poor and destitute, they had nothing except a lot of explaining to do. Slowly, they regrouped (except for Stu), and began looking for a few gigs.

The obvious place to look was Pete's mum's place, the Casbah. Mona welcomed them back graciously, and soon they were playing gigs again—but the Beatles had changed. Mona watched from the back of the hall as what appeared to be an entirely different band took the stage. Musically, they had gone through a small revolution in Hamburg and come out a rock 'n' roll band on the other side. They took the stage with force, in their ratty leather jackets, long hair, and hard attitudes, overshadowing the other bands with their stiff matching suits and clean-cut songs. In addition, they played their instruments with more confidence and more skill and actually *performed*, with ease and wit. Teenagers everywhere took notice. The Beatles had returned.

Stu was still nowhere to be found. Then word came in the mail that he was engaged to Astrid. His parents were devastated, and the band thought he had lost his mind. He eventually returned in February of 1961, though still engaged. His parents were heartbroken, while the band relentlessly made fun of him. Stu rejoined the band, although he resented them (they were the reason he had given up his art), and the feelings were becoming mutual (Stu continued to be awful on the bass and was holding them back).

The Liverpool the Beatles returned to was busy being reborn. Despite an economic downturn, a new scene had taken over the city: the "beat" scene. Music and the arts was the new thing, and the concert world was thriving. The Jac was as full as ever with artists, teddy boys, jazz players, and everyone looking for the next big thing. Allan Williams was going full tilt into the music business, even putting a large sum of his own money into renting a space to hold a week-long concert displaying local bands and beat music. Unfortunately, after five straight nights of pure mayhem and good income, the rental space burned down, leaving Allan by the wayside, a bit poorer and extremely disgruntled.

So when the Beatles approached him for work, he was in no mood to deal with them. He passed them off to his new right-hand man, Bob Wooler. Bob also appeared to be in no mood for the Beatles at the moment. Bob had had a double life: a desk clerk by day and a music-venue prowler by night, trying his hand in the scene as a promoter, emcee, DJ, and host. As it turned out, kids liked the sound of him, as Bob had a deep, harmonious voice like that of announcers they heard on the radio. He made a life introducing bands and keeping the crowd going between sets. So it was a seemingly natural career move to leave his desk job to become a full-time emcee when he ran into Allan and heard of his musical ventures.

Except that it had failed when the new venue burned down within a week. Bob, unemployed and feeling hopeless, ignored the Beatles' requests for the time being, though he did like their music and their style. Instead, he floated around Liverpool, drinking too much and checking out different venues, if only to keep himself busy and to wallow in his own misery. Then he stumbled into the Cavern, the venue where John had upset the jazz crowd by playing rock 'n' roll. At first he was taken aback by the three-story excuse for a stairwell that led him to a pit of sweat and grime. As it turned out, the Cavern had traded hands: Alan Sytner had sold it to Ray McFall, his accountant. Ray also loved jazz and attempted to keep the club strictly that, but with a failing jazz crowd, Ray began to dabble with local rock 'n' roll bands; this time, the introduction of rock 'n' roll was just what the Cavern needed.

The day that Bob found himself at the Cavern, which was supposed to be a jazz cellar, he instead found that a band called the Big Three, which he had emceed for at another hall. The place was a frenzy of heat, sweat, and music, and Bob found himself intrigued and motivated to become a part of it. As fate would have it, when the Big

Three left the stage, their drummer—recognizing Bob—stuck a microphone into his face and told him to say something. Bob switched into DJ mode and replied "Remember, all you cave dwellers, that the Cavern is the best of cellars!"[3] Ray McFall, the new owner, heard the voice over the speakers and recognized Bob from other shows he'd been to. A few days later, Ray offered Bob a permanent spot as the lunchtime DJ.

Once Bob had a job again—not to mention a job he loved—he started promoting the Beatles to Ray. Ray, a devout jazz lover, wanted nothing to do with them. But Bob would work their name into conversations and slyly mention how he'd heard they were very good, subtly getting the idea into Ray's head. Luckily for Bob and the Beatles, Ray had noticed that during lunch many young office workers would roam the streets, loitering at the music shop and outside record stores. Ray figured that if he opened up for lunch, these bored office workers just might come down for a drink and a dance. The idea had minimal risk, so long as Ray got the right bands for the crowd.

This was how the Beatles came to debut at the Cavern in early 1961. Bob's fanfare about the Beatles was true: between 50 and 60 customers came through the Cavern door that first lunch hour. The Bluegenes, the main act for lunch, were completely overshadowed by five shaggy teenagers from Liverpool. They were signed up to play three to four gigs a week, for a little over one pound each per day. Word spread quickly through Liverpool's new and growing music crowd, and soon by lunch the line to get in would stretch down the street and around the corner. Ray's prediction was more than accurate.

Playing the Cavern as a rock 'n' roll band was hard: the physical effort required to perform, combined with the tiny rotten hole the Cavern was, equaled sweat and more sweat. The bricks on the wall would run with perspiration collected from the band and the many jumping, screaming girls before them, not to mention the smell emanating from the walls, after years of smoke, booze, sweat, and hormones mingling in the cave. Still, they pushed forward, not letting a little sweat hold back their showmanship.

But while sweat didn't hold them back, Stu still was. Tension between Stu and John was so thick one could trip over it. The band carried Stu musically, but Stu was resentful of being set back in his art. It was a breakup that should have occurred far sooner than it did, especially with Paul dying to get his hands on a bass guitar. In the meantime, John and Paul would battle it out onstage—subtly of course—to be the center of attention. Neither of them seemed to notice that most of the girls only saw Pete Best, the quintessential heartthrob of the group. Privately, tension was rising, but when they hit the stage, they were completely in sync. Because of this, they carried onward, with self-centered notions kept quiet.

The Cavern was doing well for them, and they had a lot of fans, but after a little over a month they were somewhat bored with it. Wild Hamburg seemed to be beckoning them back, after having ended so quickly, so Pete Best made a quick call to Peter Eckhorn, at the Top Ten Club. He immediately booked them, offering them twice what they had received at the Kaiserkeller. On top of that, since Pete made the call, they felt they didn't owe Allan Williams at Jacaranda Enterprises his 10 percent cut.

In the spring of 1961, the five returned to Germany, this time with proper permits. The gig at the Top Ten turned out to be even more demanding than the Kaiserkeller: the hours were longer, beginning at 7 P.M. and going until 3 A.M., and the Top Ten was massive, so the need to "make show" was all the more necessary. Upon being reunited with Astrid, however, Stu became increasingly frustrated with the band: Paul taunted him ceaselessly, even to the point of violence, and John seemed completely indifferent to Stu's existence. Stu complained about all this to Astrid, and she suggested he try returning to art. Some of her friends attended the Hamburg State Art College— which had recently acquired a famous sculptor, and one of Stu's idols, as one of their professors: Edouardo Paolozzi. Stu took a few of his samples to Edouardo, who accepted him immediately into his program and managed to get Stu a grant as well. For a while Stu attempted to lead both lives: he would play with the band until 3 A.M., then go to his attic and paint until dawn. Without sleep he would then attend class, kept awake by booze and pills. Slowly, art won Stu's heart back, and he drifted away from the Beatles, leaving the position of bass player open, which Paul quickly claimed.

As one last hurrah, Stu announced he would be the one to write to Allan Williams about the loss of his 10 percent commission—a job that had been avoided by all, probably because each of them knew Allan didn't deserve to be treated so harshly. But the letter was sent nonetheless, as 10 percent was a lot of money to them at that time, and Allan wrote back a deservingly angry and threatening letter, denying them any chances to redeem themselves. The Beatles were swiftly dropped from Allan's management.

The Beatles: from left, Paul McCartney, Ringo Starr, John Lennon, and George Harrison are shown rehearsing in a studio in London, England. October 1, 1963. (AP Photo)

Their time in Hamburg was crucial to their development as a band. Their music repertoire grew rapidly, as did their stage presence, and their look. It was Astrid who had a hand in the Beatles' look, cutting their hair and helping them pick clothes, thereby lighting the fuse that would one day rocket them to fame. Astrid played hairdresser, and she shaped their long locks into what would come to be known as the "mop top." Over the course of their time in Hamburg, their iconic look was developed, alongside their performance skills, their endurance skills, and their musical abilities. "In my opinion, our peak for playing live was in Hamburg because at that time we weren't famous," said George, "The Hamburg days, in retrospect, were probably the most important times of our lives because it was . . . our apprenticeship."[4]

Also during this stint in Hamburg, a German orchestra leader and producer for a German record label called Polydor, named Bert Kaempfert, showed up on the scene. He was looking for bands to record cheesy cover songs, the kind that would appeal to the German middle class out for a night at the pub. He hired Tony Sheridan and the Beatles to record them.

The songs were awful, but the Beatles were thrilled to be in the same room as recording equipment and didn't complain at all. Bert renamed them the Beat Brothers for the recording and chose the songs "My Bonnie Lies over the Ocean" and "When the Saints Go Marching In" to be recorded. Although the songs chosen were obviously not the kind the Beatles would choose, they performed them well. Bert was impressed with the Beatles and let them privately cut two extra songs of their choosing for the album. They recorded "Ain't She Sweet" as a group, and an instrumental by George called "Cry for a Shadow." Polydor retained the rights to these songs. This would be the first album recorded by the Beatles.

Burned out from the Top Ten Club, and having successfully recorded a record, the Beatles called it a day and returned to Liverpool in June 1961. Stu stayed behind, to marry Astrid and continue studying with Edouardo. The four remaining musicians caught the train home to once again find Liverpool a very different place.

Rock 'n' roll music had exploded all over Liverpool like a bomb, and jazz, which had been the long-time Liverpool favorite, was nearly decimated in the attack, with jazz bars closing almost as fast as rock 'n' roll clubs were popping up. Formal dance clubs, featuring ballroom and quickstep, were also shutting down as pop and rock venues swung open their doors, sometimes holding dances all night long. Beat music, as it was called, took over the city and claimed it within months. Along with new venues, a brilliant idea was born by Bill Harry, the schoolmate who had dubbed John a teddy boy on his first day at the Liverpool Institute, and had introduced John to Stu. Bill was very much involved in the music scene in Liverpool and he knew exactly where and when everyone was playing, although he noticed that other fans would often not know when their favorite group would be playing next. His great idea would prove ingenious: a newspaper devoted to music.

Dubbed *Mersey Beat*, Bill Harry ran the whole paper on his own, with his girlfriend Virginia as a secretary. Bill still considered John a good friend and gave the Beatles lots of room in the paper, publishing some of Astrid's photos and even having John—against his will—write some articles. The first edition ran at 5,000 copies, all of which immediately sold out. Advertisers were eager to get their ad in the paper, and the North End Music Store (NEMS) was among the first. The ad, and a short article, discussed the records that the NEMS store had for sale and encouraged people to come take a look. The article was written by co-owner of the store and future manager of the Beatles' Brian Epstein.

* * *

Brian Epstein was the eldest son of Malka, called Queenie, and Harry Epstein, born on September 19, 1934. Queenie and Harry both came from prominent Jewish families, both of which owned respected furniture stores, and Harry continued with the family business. The Epsteins' shop was on Walton Road, right next to NEMS, where Jim McCartney had once purchased his family's piano. Eventually the Epsteins took over NEMS, to expand their inventory from furniture to radios and music.

Brian grew up in a lavish lifestyle and took after his mother's passion for theater and the arts. He was kicked out of many schools, however, for being a problem child who was constantly in trouble. While Queenie knew her son was a bit rambunctious, she also knew that anti-Semitism still ran strong in Liverpool. Hopeful, she continued to place Brian in school after school, finally ending up at Wrekin, in Dorset. There, though it was a strict boys' school, he did well in art and acting, and this held his attention for a while, but at age 15, Brian dropped out of school altogether. When Queenie begged him for a reason, he announced to his family that he did not need school for his chosen profession: he was going to London and become a dress designer.

The Epstein family was hardworking and straight-edged, and dress designing did not sit well with them. They forbade him to go to London and also ruled out art school, where Brian wanted to pursue theater and acting. Not wanting to return to regular school, and forbidden from pursuing fashion or art, Brian eventually caved in to his parents' desire: he began to work at the family store.

As it turned out, Brian was a natural salesperson, constantly persuading people to spend more than they needed to. Brian thrived, and he also took to overseeing the window dressing and creating wild displays. This upset his grandfather, who was very old-fashioned, and the two argued regularly. Brian's father, Harry, decided to separate them and sent Brian to the store's Liverpool branch.

There, Brian was the ultimate bachelor: born and raised in money, a natural salesman, and with a taste for luxury and fine clothes. Fashionable and witty, Brian was popular within his circles, and women flocked to him. Unfortunately for them, Brian was utterly and completely homosexual. Facing his sexuality was a battle that would last most of his life. In the 1950s, this was still illegal and totally taboo, and tolerance was unheard of. So, to be safe, he kept this information to himself and tried to fly under the radar.

Alas, Brian was not the best at hiding. On a whim, he auditioned for a playhouse and was accepted. Not a very good actor, but admired and liked by his peers, Brian stepped further in the theater world— the one place where homosexuality might be tolerated, and where other homosexuals might be found. Whether or not Brian was on the prowl, he used the washroom one night at a theater and had a mildly flirtatious conversation with the man next to him. It was, as it turned out, an undercover cop trying to lure and bust homosexuals. Having done nothing wrong, Brian was still charged with importuning the officer.

Luckily, Brian's parents never heard anything of it. Brian worked hard by day but continued to seek out company at night, even though it risked arrest and violence. One day in 1958 he struck up a conversation with another young man hiding in the shadows. When Brian saw the man, he was shocked. It was Joe Flannery, his childhood best friend. The two of them began a love affair, with Brian often turning up at Joe's beaten and bleeding after a night on the streets trying to pick up other men. One might even conclude that Brian enjoyed the threat, the chase, the violence—it excited him. Joe patiently took care of him, despite this.

In 1958, Harry Epstein opened another store in central Liverpool. He called it NEMS, like the other music shop, and Brian ran the music department, while his younger brother Clive ran the furniture section. Brian, a lover of the arts, took it upon himself to make the music section a success. He could never have dreamed how far it would end up taking him.

NOTES

1. Philip Norman, *John Lennon: The Life* (New York: Doubleday Canada. 2008), 198.
2. David Pritchard and Alan Lysaght, *The Beatles: An Oral History* (Toronto: Soddart Publishing, 1998), 50.
3. Quoted in Philip Norman, *Shout! The Beatles in Their Generation* (New York: Simon & Schuster, 2005), 109.
4. Quoted in David Pritchard and Alan Lysaght, *The Beatles: An Oral History* (Toronto: Soddart Publishing, 1998), 51.

CHAPTER FIVE

As Big As Elvis

Gentlemen, you have just recorded your first number one.

George Martin

By 1961, the music industry was experiencing a massive boom in popularity. Therefore, Brian Epstein made every effort to have the most well-stocked record collection in Liverpool, since there was much competition. One of Brian's rules for his NEMS shop was to never turn down a customer: if he didn't have the record someone was looking for, he would order it immediately.

On October 28, a young man named Raymond Jones strolled into Brian's store looking for a record no one there had heard of: "My Bonnie" by the Beatles. Raymond had no clue which record company had recorded it but told Brian that the band was local, played lunch hours down at the Cavern, and that the DJ, Bob Wooler, had told the crowd to go out and ask for their single. Brian couldn't find the name in any of his books, or in his stocks, but he stayed true to his policy: the record would be ordered.

Brian's ego was slightly bruised, as he prided himself as a music man who knew all the bands in town and the big names abroad. He was only 27 years old and did not enjoy feeling "out of the loop." He began to hunt down the Beatles' record, but to no avail. Not a single record company or supplier had heard of them or recorded their music (of course, this is because they had recorded in Germany and under the name the Beat Brothers).

Most might have given up the search, but Brian was intrigued. On November 9, 1961, he discovered that the Cavern Club was just two blocks from his store. Brian immediately went down at lunchtime with his assistant, Alistair Taylor, to track down the Beatles and find out where on earth they had recorded this single. Brian felt violated by the foul stench of the Cavern, seemed about 10 years too old to be there, and was certainly overdressed, but something made him stay regardless.

Brian was amused as the Beatles fooled around on stage, pushing, laughing, joking, and being all-around cocky. But then they launched into their songs, and Brian was hooked. They weren't just messing around—they were good. They rocked around the stage with catchy riffs, harmonies, and tight timing, delivering song after song at a furious pace. And considering Brian's hidden sexuality, it didn't hurt that they were four handsome, skinny young men clad in leather and long hair, sweating and thrashing around on stage. Between sets he managed to find out they recorded overseas with Polydor, and later he emerged back into the daylight, now a different man with new ideas.

Brian continued to visit the Beatles at lunchtime throughout November, asking around about how much they made, who managed them, and where they played at night. The Beatles were flattered, although confused, about what a nice young businessman like Mr. Epstein would want with them. What they didn't know was that Brian had made to himself the seemingly ridiculous decision to manage the Beatles. Brian didn't have any experience for the job, but he did have connections, resources, and enough charm to sell anything to anybody.

Brian met with the Beatles twice in December, and during the second meeting he laid out his idea to manage them. There were a few minutes of silence as they let the idea sink in: a millionaire, with connections to record companies, wanted to manage them. One might think an appropriate reaction would be to jump up and down and scream with excitement, but the Beatles were far too cool to let that happen, for now. They carefully agreed, so long as their music remained untouched.

Brian immediately did two things: first, being a gentleman, he paid individual visits to all of the parents to explain his intentions and plans. The parents were unsure at first, but they were easily swayed by

Brian's natural charm, soothingly posh accent, and impeccable manners. Second, Brian began trying to get them a record deal. With NEMS being a massive record retailer, he had solid working relationships with all the major record companies, like Decca, Phillips, and EMI. The first to respond was Decca, which, probably just to be polite, sent a young representative named Mike Smith up to hear the Beatles play. Mike was impressed, enough to ask them for a second audition in London, which was scheduled to take place on January 1, 1962.

After a long day of getting lost in blizzards on their way to London, on the morning of January 1 the Beatles were beyond nervous. Mike Smith arrived late and hastily set them to work. They played 15 songs, ranging from covers to originals, ready to play whatever it took to win Mike over. However, the anxiety got to them, and they performed poorly: George's hand cramped up, Paul's voice cracked, and John forgot words. Mike assured them they played fine, but he had to choose between them and another group who had performed better. In the end, Mike—a new employee—played it on the safe side and went with the second group.

Brian was furious. He returned to London and demanded to meet with the higher-ups. He was told that groups with guitars were "on the way out."[1] Brian continued fighting with Decca about the decision, finally giving up and announcing that the Beatles would, one day, be "bigger than Elvis,"[2] only to be met with laughter.

Though he was busy with record companies, Brian still took time to teach the band some lessons on professionalism. No more being late—punctuality was professional. No more unrehearsed shows—there must be a program of songs. No more eating and drinking during a set. No more shouting, swearing, or joking with the audience between songs. No going onstage until all members were present. Most importantly—no more leather. The band had been in the same suits since Germany and smelled as bad as the Cavern. In essence, they were forced to go from ragamuffin Scousers to professional musicians.

During January of 1962, Brian formed a limited company to oversee the costs and profits of the Beatles. He called it NEMS Enterprises, after his store. Brian then took to arranging their local shows. When he had time, he would return to London to barter with the record companies, again and again. And when he wasn't doing those things, he was still running NEMS five days a week. It quickly became too much for him.

As fate would have it, Brian was out with the band one night when an old friend—and lover—walked in. Joe Flannery spotted Brian and came over to say hello; they had not seen each other in five years. Brian introduced Joe to each of the band members, and then he and Joe went off alone to catch up. It turned out that Joe was also managing a band that his younger brother was in: Lee Curtis and the All Stars. Joe, still in love with Brian, offered to work for him and help take the pressure off booking so many small-time local shows.

Joe began observing John Lennon. He noticed how abrasive and harsh John was, to his band mates, and to Brian. He was snarky, mean, selfish, and proud; he was even borderline violent sometimes, pushing and kicking people at his whim. He was exactly the kind of man Brian had been attracted to all those late nights out on the streets, coming home beat up and broken. Why Brian had such a strange attraction to violent and abrasive men, Joe couldn't understand. But he did understand this: Brian was in love with John Lennon.

It didn't take Joe long to figure it out. Brian, ever so confident and charming, would stutter and turn red when speaking to John. John had noticed this, and instead of giving the man a break, he would stare him down during conversations, causing Brian to nearly fall over with nerves. John was also harsh with his words, and very sarcastic toward Brian. Joe spent many nights in a car, consoling Brian as he cried over something John had said.

Regardless of whatever was going on between Brian and John, life as band and manager continued. Brian spent his time nagging London and bothering everyone he could think of to give the Beatles a chance. John and the band continued to play gigs—although now they wore matching silver suits and tried to be on time. Joe continued booking gigs and helping with the behind-the-scenes work of running a band. Brian tried to keep the group's heads up by always acting positive and saying opportunities were knocking. He forced Joe to "interrupt" a meeting and say that Elvis's manager was trying to get hold of him. They bought it, and that bought Brian more time to figure out what on earth to do next. With no recording opportunities on the horizon, all Brian could come up with was to send them back to Germany.

***

At the same time that Brian was working so hard to keep the Beatles' popularity alive, a former Beatle was dying. Stu Sutcliffe had been attending art school in Germany and spending days at a time painting, often without so much as food or sleep; he was also plagued by raging headaches. He began collapsing during school and appeared gaunt and ghostlike. His mother, Millie, was certain her son was sick; unfortunately, she was right.

The Christmas of 1961, Stu and Astrid returned to Liverpool, and Millie almost immediately began taking Stu to the hospital for tests, but nothing could be found. Stu, however, continued going downhill, his headache symptoms worsening to include temporary blindness and blackouts. He had to return to Hamburg to continue with school, and by March 1962, he wavered constantly between raging pain and complete normalcy. He knew the Beatles were returning to Hamburg for a show on April 13 and looked forward to it greatly.

However, on April 10, Astrid's mother sent Stu to the hospital, finding him worse than ever. Astrid was in the ambulance, and Stu passed away in her arms. Millie Sutcliffe was informed by telegram later that day. That same day, the Beatles were headed to Hamburg, this time by airplane, without any idea of Stu's death. Their flight turned out to be the same one Millie had booked at the last minute. She tearfully broke the news during the flight.

As it turned out, Stu had had a small tumor in his brain. This was amplified by a depression in his skull, which pressed down on the tumor and caused all of those headaches and blackouts. Millie blamed in on all the nights the band had been beaten up, mostly one particular night that Stu had been kicked in the head repeatedly, coming home covered in blood. Stu had decided at the time that he was too busy to go to the hospital, and instead he resumed his studies with his head unchecked.

Even though the rest of the band, except for John, couldn't stop crying about Stu, they still had to perform that night. The Star Club was the newest club in Hamburg, overshadowing the Kaiserkeller and the Top Ten Club. It was said that as many as 15 to 18 thousand people could pass through it in a single day, as it was open from 4 P.M. to 6 A.M. It was a gig that couldn't afford to be messed up, so they put on their best faces and delivered the lively performance they had become known for. John and Astrid would spend the late nights talking about Stu. John, when he let his guard down, would waiver between affection and nostalgia, then anger and resentment (probably due to his deep-seated fear of abandonment). Astrid continued to watch them play at night, to avoid being alone with her overwhelming sense of emptiness. The band played day and night at the Star Club, once again full of pills and booze to keep them going, and to drown out the sorrow of Stu's untimely demise.

Meanwhile, Brian continued his relentless pursuit of record companies. He was hardly ever at NEMS, his real job, despite his promise that he would only work with the Beatles two afternoons a week. By now, he was lucky if he made it in for half his shifts. The main reason was that his trips to London were almost weekly. During one such trip someone suggested to Brian that he transfer the Beatles' demo from tape to disc, for better quality and a more professional impression. So, while in London, Brian met up with a studio engineer named Jim Foye, who did just that. Jim liked the Beatles, he thought they had something going, and he offered to play the new disc to the studio's boss, Syd Colmen. Syd, as well, enjoyed the sound on the disc and was impressed with the band, even if the recording wasn't great. EMI's two major labels, Columbia and HMV, had already turned down the Beatles, so Syd sent Brian to a smaller branch of EMI, Parlophone.

Brian went to Parlophone, where he met with their record producer George Martin. George, like Brian, was a charming man with a handsome and regal disposition. The two liked each other immediately, and George agreed to have the Beatles audition. Brian sent a telegram to the Beatles in Hamburg: CONGRATULATIONS BOYS, EMI REQUESTS RECORDING SESSION. PLEASE REHEARSE NEW MATERIAL.[3] Though Brian had only arranged an audition, the wording of the telegram led the Beatles to believe they would be recording. Of course, Brian often overstated things: this was the same man who had convinced them Elvis's manager was calling.

The historic audition took place June 6, 1962, at EMI's Abbey Road Studios in St. John's Wood. George thoroughly tested each of the band members for ability and variety, hoping perhaps to find, at the very least, a solo performer, which was a popular trend at the time. He was not very impressed with the selection of songs Brian had picked out, and he was even less impressed with their original music. Most of all, he was unhappy with Pete Best's drumming. By the end of the summer of 1962, George Martin offered them a chance to record a single on one stipulation: fire Pete Best.

It had been coming for a while, as Pete just didn't quite fit in with the others: his hair was short, he was utterly handsome in a very classic way, and, still abstaining from the pep pills, he simply couldn't keep up with the pace of the band. It was Brian who ended it, calling Pete to his office the morning of August 16. Pete was absolutely blindsided. Brian attempted to console Pete with offers of making him another group, but Pete wanted nothing to do with any of them.

He and his best friend Neil went straight to a pub and got drunk. Pete cut himself off from the Beatles, refusing to play at their show that very night. Pete would go on to become a baker and marry a nice girl named Kathy. The Beatles would go on to become legends.

Although they had lost Pete Best, they hadn't lost Pete's most valuable asset: Neil Aspinall. Neil was Pete's best friend and was planning on becoming an accountant, but he had a soft spot for music and had been the band's faithful roadie and chauffeur ever since Pete had joined. When Pete was kicked out, Neil offered to go too, but Pete gave his blessing for Neil to stay if he wanted. By then, the Beatles had come to rely on Neil for many things, and they would never have been able to carry on without him. Knowing this, Neil stayed.

The Beatles continued to gain popularity. Earlier that year, they had been voted by *Mersey Beat* as the most popular band of 1961, and they were known all across Liverpool. And of course, they continued to be infamous in Hamburg. With the popularity came girls. One night Cynthia was with Dot when Paul showed up unexpectedly. He announced to Dot that too many girls were after him and he no longer wanted to be tied down to just one. Paul left, and Cynthia consoled Dot, while silently wondering what her own fate would be.

Fate had a different plan for her. That August, while the band ditched Pete and signed a recording contract, Cynthia discovered she was pregnant. It was just luck that she hadn't gotten pregnant sooner, as she and John had never used birth control during their relationship of more than two years. She told John, through many tears, awaiting his most-likely disastrous response. To her surprise, John asked her to marry him. He said it was the right thing to do.

Cynthia's mother had been away in Canada all summer, and she was home for a short period of time before returning to Canada again. Cynthia confessed to her the day before her mother was due to leave, but she also announced that she and John would get married. Cynthia's mother agreed this was the best plan, but at the same time, she refused to extend her stay to attend the wedding. John went to Mimi and told her the same story. Mimi was furious; she couldn't stand watching John make the same mistake his mother had, getting married so young, and on a whim. She refused to attend the wedding or even give her blessing to them.

John and Cynthia were married at the Mount Pleasant Register Office, August 24, 1962, with no parents to witness the wedding, just as Julia Lennon had in 1938. John was 22; Cynthia was 23. Cynthia's brother gave her away, her sister was her bridesmaid, and Brian stood by John as his best man. It was pouring rain, and there was road work taking place outside the office, so most of the ceremony was inaudible. George and Paul giggled, and Cynthia wore secondhand clothes, unable to afford a new wedding outfit. Afterward, they went for lunch across the street. Brian paid, and as a gift, he told John and Cynthia they could use his private flat for as long as they needed. One stipulation though: the marriage, and the pregnancy, needed to stay secret. Brian was terrified that female fans would be put off if they found out John had a wife and child, that it would ruin the image of the band as four young, carefree, rebellious lads. In her usual way, Cynthia agreed.

One day before the wedding, *Mersey Beat* had announced that the Beatles had fired Pete Best. There were uproars everywhere; petitions were signed and letters poured in. Girls even took to the street protesting with signs. But this was the least of Brian's concerns: he needed a new drummer. This led to the theft of Ringo Starr.

***

Ringo was born Richard Starkey Jr., on July 7, 1940, to Elsie Gleave and Richard Starkey Sr. His family lived in shanty town in Liverpool called Dingle. It was, to be blunt, a slum. Shortly after his birth, Richard Sr. took off, never to be heard from again, except for a few months of support payments. Elsie took a job as a barmaid and eventually was remarried to Harry Greaves, the closest thing Ringo, then called Ritchie, would have as a father.

He was a happy child, but constantly ill. At six, his appendix burst and peritonitis set in rapidly. Ritchie spent over three months in a coma, and more than a year in the hospital. When he finally returned to school, he could not read or write, having fallen so far behind. At 13, a cold become pleurisy and affected his lungs greatly. He went to the Heswall Children's Hospital, where he stayed for the next two years. He would never return to school.

In 1956, when the skiffle craze hit, Ritchie took up drums to join in. He played with a band in the hospital ward and later formed a group with a friend, working the same skiffle halls as the Quarrymen had. However, where the Quarrymen had failed, Ritchie had succeeded as a professional drummer, landing a gig with Rory Storm and the Hurricanes and earning the nickname "Ringo" due to wearing so many rings on his fingers. When both bands ended up in Hamburg together, the Beatles had seen and heard what a good drummer Ringo was. He had been on their minds ever since.

He was not easy to track down, but John finally found him and offered him 25 pounds a week to play with the Beatles. Luckily for John, Rory Storm's popularity had been decreasing lately, and Ringo was already wondering what to do next. Ringo agreed and was effectively stolen from Rory Storm. The Beatles were thrilled. Rory was furious.

The Beatles, minus Pete, plus Ringo, turned up on September 11, 1962, to record with George Martin, at his studio on Abbey Road, with Ringo Starr in tow. George, not knowing they had found a new drummer, had brought in a session drummer already, named Andy White. George struck a deal that both of them would drum for each song, recording the song twice, and the best version would make the cut. In the end, they recorded so many times that no one really knows who is drumming on the album. Regardless, a single was cut. George chose "Love Me Do" for the A side and "P.S. I Love You" for the B side.

On October 1, the Beatles signed a five-year contract with Brian Epstein, never guessing what lay ahead in those long five years. Then, on October 4, the Beatles' first single was released, although it was met with laughter and mocking down at EMI. Brian, seeing he had no support in London, immediately purchased 10,000 copies of the record for NEMS. He then turned to the Beatles' fans and began to campaign for letters to Radio Luxembourg, and the BBC. Family, friends, and nearly anyone who had ever seen, met, or known the Beatles (except, perhaps, Pete Best) began to write letters to any and every radio station, demanding "Love Me Do" be played.

That September, Brian had come up with a strategy to boost the band's popularity. Through NEMS he began bringing in more popular bands and having the Beatles come second on the lineup. Some big name would headline the poster, and the Beatles would go second, followed by other bands down the line. This seemed to work better than trying to have the Beatles as the headliners. In a great feat, Brian, using all of his sway as manager of NEMS, managed to book the infamous Little Richard.

As if in a dream, on October 12 the band took the stage to open for one of their long-time idols. The concert was held at a venue called New Brighton Tower, with even more bands than Allan Williams had booked years before (where the Beatles had sat, humiliated, next to the stage). Little Richard—who was infamous due to his violent, outrageous, unpredictable personality—was an angel, amicable and agreeable with everyone. The Beatles were a hit and nearly passed out when Little Richard came to talk with them. It was then that Little Richard taught Paul McCartney how to make his trademark "Ooooh!" "When I first saw the Beatles, I didn't think they'd make it," said Little Richard, later, "[Paul] wanted to learn my little holler, so we sat at the piano going, 'ooooh!' until he got it."[4]

After being buried in letters from fans, Radio Luxembourg relented and played the song; the BBC followed suit shortly after. Requests continued to pour in. And then, it happened: there, at number 49 on the charts, it read "The Beatles." They had made the top 100. And, even more exciting, the song continued to climb. Slowly, but surely, by December 13, the song rose to number 17. They had made the top 20.

George Martin immediately called them in to record a second single. In the meantime, the band piled into the studio and recorded "Please Please Me" on November 26. As they played, their voices soared in harmony, and the catchiness of both the tune, and the band, came together in a combustible manner. George was stunned. After the first take he announced into the intercom, "Gentlemen, you have just recorded your first number one."[5] Knowing the song was a hit, Brian decided to ditch EMI for their complete lack of help with "Love Me Do" and opted for a new publisher. George suggested an ambitious man named Dick James. Brian and Dick met the next day, and after Dick showed off his impressive connections, Brian was sold and allowed Dick James Music to publish the new song.

The year came to an end with the Beatles returning to Hamburg for a two-week stint in their old stomping grounds. They took the stage at the Star Club on December 31, 1962, properly inebriated, and said goodbye to the place that had given birth to their sound, had raised them, and had refined them. They left Hamburg, unaware that they would never be back, not in the same way. In fact, come 1963, nothing would ever be the same again.

***

"Please Please Me" was released in the United Kingdom on January 11, 1963, with high hopes for the New Year. Things were looking good when the Beatles appeared on the second most popular TV show in the United Kingdom, called *Thank Your Lucky Stars*. This had been set up by Dick James in the fall, as a show of good faith to Brian, and to secure the Beatles under his publishing company. They performed "Please Please Me" on January 13, 1963, and it aired later that week. The snowfall was heavy, which proved to be great luck for the band, as many teenagers were at home, snowed in and bored, watching the show.

With the new single out, the band hit the road right away, opening for a teenage sensation, Helen Shapiro. It was a cold and icy winter—the worst one to hit the area in nearly a hundred years—and it was spent in a van touring from town to town. While the band was busy touring, "Please Please Me" was climbing the charts. It entered at number 47, then 39, and then 21. Finally, after four weeks, it happened: "Please Please Me" by the Beatles was number one.

Once again, the band immediately went back into the studio. In one 13-hour marathon of a recording session, they recorded an entire album: *Please Please Me*, with a whopping 14 songs, including "I Saw Her Standing There," "P.S. I Love You," all the current singles, and a feisty cover of "Twist and Shout." On March 22, the album was in stores.

The Beatles' first album went straight to the top of the charts. Within two weeks, 250,000 copies of *Please Please Me* had been sold, at a time when albums sold minimally. A new single was released on April 11, "From Me to You." The B-side was "Thank You Girl" and "The One After 909." Within two weeks, "From Me to You" was number one.

The same month, on April 8, Cynthia Lennon gave birth to a baby boy, whom she named John Charles Julian Lennon. He would be called Julian, after Julia Lennon. As John held Julian for the first time he exclaimed, "Cyn, he's bloody marvellous!"[6] John was beaming, and Cynthia was pleased as punch just to see John, who had been away on tour so long, and to see him happy with his son. She was less pleased when John announced he would be taking a vacation soon, that very month. She was thoroughly displeased when John told her this trip was to Spain, with Brian Epstein. Alone.

Cynthia was both hurt and helpless: hurt that John would go away after the birth, leaving her alone to tend to a new baby; helpless to do anything about it. But she knew he deserved a break, so she gave him her blessing. Without her husband, Cynthia went home to Aunt Mimi's, where she had moved in during the pregnancy, tired of being alone at Brian's flat all day. As she cradled her son and hid from fans who pooled outside Mimi's house hoping for a glimpse of John, John was flying away to Barcelona with Brian.

What transpired on the trip remains between Brian and John. When they returned home, rumors were flying within the band's circle about the two of them, mostly having to do with their potentially sexual relationship. Unconcerned about the rumors, Brian and John remained amicable and businesslike upon their return; that is, until Paul's 21st birthday. There, Bob Wooler teased John about it, and John attacked him, breaking several ribs before being pulled away. From then on, nobody in the Beatles circle would comment on Brian and John's relationship.

NOTES

1. Quoted in Philip Norman, *Shout! The Beatles in Their Generation* (New York: Simon & Schuster, 2005), 153.
2. Ibid, 153.
3. Quoted in Peter Brown and Steven Gaines, *The Love You Make: An Insider's Story of the Beatles* (New York: McGraw-Hill Book Company, 1976), 77.
4. Quoted in Keith Badman, *The Beatles: Off the Record* (New York: Music Sales Corp, 2000), 45.
5. Quoted in Brown and Gaines, *The Love You Make*, 89.
6. Quoted in Cynthia Lennon, *John* (New York: Random House, 2005), 155–56.

CHAPTER SIX

Beatlemania!

We don't think the Beatles will do anything in this market.
                                                                    Capitol Records

During this time of such success, with three songs breaking the top
20 and two going to number one, Brian decided to keep cashing in by
signing other Liverpool groups. He started with Gerry and the Pacemakers. Once Gerry and the Pacemakers hit number one and there
were two bands from the same town enjoying such success, the term
"Mersey sound" was coined, and any band from Liverpool or the area
was dubbed with it. Brian continued to sign bands, such as a handsome young crooner he named Billy J. Kramer, and another popular
Cavern group, the Big Three. He then took on Priscilla White, the
coat-check girl from the Cavern. They dubbed her Cilla Black, and
soon she was also on her way to becoming a star. With five bands
under his belt, Brian opened up another NEMS office in London
and moved there to tend to his goals of attaining world fame and
making money. He set the bands up recording Lennon-McCartney
songs—as they seemed to have an endless supply and more turning
up each week—and soon the Top 20 was dominated by NEMS acts.
In essence, the Beatles had sung or written nearly all the songs in the
top 10 at that time.

He left the NEMS in central Liverpool to be run by his associate Peter Brown. He then hired a publicist, Tony Barrow, to work in the London office with him. With the fame of his bands, especially the Beatles—for whom thousands of love letters poured in daily—he took on a second publicist, a young man named Andrew Loog Oldham, who had previously worked for Larry Parnes. Andrew wanted work with the Beatles but ended up overseeing the other bands, which he grew quickly bored of. Andrew got a tip about an up-and-coming band and went to go scout them on his own. The band played a strange adaptation of rhythm and blues, and the lead singer was a gangly economics student, but the band had something, something really big. Andrew approached Brian about this and offered him 50 percent of the band in exchange for an investment. Brian declined. This is how it came to pass that Brian Epstein turned down the Rolling Stones, and a chance to manage two of the greatest bands in rock history.

Meanwhile, the spring and summer of 1963 flew by in a daze: tour after tour, each and every day was filled with appearances and shows, and the long open road between towns. John hardly had time to even take it all in now that he had a son. On August 3, the band played their final night at the Cavern, bidding it adieu just as they had Hamburg. On August 23, they released their fourth single, "She Loves You" / "I'll Get You" and it went straight to number one nearly overnight. The band had a hot streak that they intended to ride as long as possible.

Harnessing the hot streak was getting easier. In September, Brian was able to get the band on the number-one TV show in the United Kingdom, *Sunday Night at the Palladium*. The show aired October 13, and an unprecedented and unbelievable 15 million viewers watched, the most ever at that time.

The band was invited to play the Royal Command Variety Performance, an annual charity gala hosted by the royal family, and among those attending would be the royal family themselves. Playing for the royal family would give them a status, beyond any doubt, as real, respectable musicians, worthy of fame. They had two weeks to get ready for the show—but alas, those two weeks would be busy, as Brian had arranged for all of them to come join him in London, permanently.

The NEMS office was on Argyll Street, near the London Palladium, in an area called Nemporer, which pleased Brian because it sort of matched the name of the company, NEMS. Brian's apartment was in an area called Knightsbridge, where he occupied a two-bedroom flat. George and Ringo moved into the same building, two floors down. This both excited and worried Brian: excited to have the boys near, worried they might catch him in the act, and discover his sexual perversions (as if they didn't already know). George and Ringo knew this, and so began "dropping in" on Brian at all hours, just to scare him. John and Cynthia moved into a flat in Kensington, on the top floor, which meant six flights up with no elevator for Cynthia and the baby. Fans quickly discovered the whereabouts of George and Ringo, and John and Cynthia, and took to camping out front all day long. Cynthia would look out her window to see banners hanging from the youth hostel across the street, bidding her husband good morning, or welcome home, or their undying love.

The only Beatle that couldn't be tracked down was Paul. As it turned out, Paul—who had been the ringleader in what was called the "bird scene," bringing multiple girls backstage or to his hotel nearly every night—had fallen in love, hard. Months earlier, Paul and the others had been introduced to a young actress named Jane Asher. All of them had instantly offered themselves to her, but Jane was a classy girl and turned each of them down. This intrigued Paul in a way that no other girl had. The others, sensing Paul's intentions, left them alone, sitting on the floor talking. They returned hours later only to find Paul and Jane in the same place, fully clothed, still talking. This was not Paul-like behavior.

Jane fascinated him. She was only 17, and stunning, with flowing red hair. She was also chaste, and a virgin, and had no interest in having Paul take that away. This only intrigued Paul more, as he was used to girls ready to throw themselves on a bed as soon as he winked. Jane was from a good family from London, a smart family that read books and had long discussions at dinner and understood world affairs of all sorts. Paul renounced his promiscuous ways and immediately became faithful and committed to Jane and Jane only, even giving up his seemingly insatiable sexual appetite out of respect for her beliefs. One night, after another long night of talking with Jane, Paul missed his flight to Liverpool, and her family offered him their spare room. Paul moved in, and stayed for two years, which is how he went virtually unnoticed by fans and the press alike.

After a five-day tour in Sweden, the Beatles returned to their new homes in London on October 29 to a very surprising scene. They were greeted by hundreds and hundreds of girls, screaming and jumping up and down on the airport's roof. Coincidentally, an American icon was visiting Europe and happened to be at Heathrow during the chaos that day. He was intrigued by all the commotion and felt that the Beatles would make a good appearance on his show: that is, *The Ed Sullivan Show*. Ed requested to meet the band and was impressed with their demeanor—and offered them a spot on his show. They agreed sometime in the early New Year would be good, and the deal was made. The Beatles would go to America.

On November 4, they went to play at the Royal Command Variety Performance. That particular night the queen could not attend, as she was very pregnant with Prince Edward, but the royal box still contained Queen Elizabeth (the queen mother) and Princess Margaret. The Beatles were part of a 19-act show and went on near the end, for four songs. They were terrified by the social status of the audience, not to mention the royal family, and Brian was terrified that John might offend someone, or everyone, with a one-liner. However, the band went on, and they stole the show—even stiff-necked businessmen and their tight-lipped wives could not resist the Beatles' charm, which they laid on thick, with a bit of cheekiness sprinkled on top very carefully. John announced their final song, "Twist and Shout," and asked the audience, "Will people in the cheaper seats clap your hands? All the rest of you, if you'll just rattle your jewellery . . ."[1] which caused the whole audience to burst into laughter.

The Daily Express headline the next day read: "Beatles Rock the Royals," while the *Daily Mail* read "Night of Triumph for Four Young Men." However, it was the headline of the *Daily Mirror*, which simply read "Beatlemania!," giving rise to the term that would follow the Beatles everywhere they went. And the mania would only continue as the band entered the recording studio again, to prepare a second album.

While the cover of *Please Please Me* had been the image of four cheeky boys grinning down from an industrial stairwell—marketing the working-class image, instead of hiding it—the album cover for their newest release was far more mature. In the same way that Astrid had played with light and dark over their faces back in Hamburg, the new album, titled *With the Beatles*, had four floating heads, each one divided in half by shadow. It was dark, mysterious, and enticing. It was arty and sophisticated, and unlike any other album cover of its time. Not only that, it was also probably the first full-length album to be released not just to highlight one or two singles, but for its entirety: every song counted. Never before had an entire album been exalted, because never before had anyone really put any effort into the songs that weren't expected to be singles.

With the Beatles was released on November 22. One week later, their fifth single was released, "I Want to Hold Your Hand." It went immediately to number one without stopping, due to more than one million advanced orders. The album also included a number of Lennon–McCartney songs, such as "All My Loving" and "It Won't Be Long," as well as a number of well-executed covers such as "Roll Over Beethoven."

With the United Kingdom thoroughly won over, Brian began his plans for taking over America. The main goal was to get a single released there, so that they could tour after appearing on *The Ed Sullivan Show*. In 1963, George Martin had been contacting the American branches of EMI several times, with various singles that were dominating the British charts, but no one in New York had been interested. "We don't think the Beatles will do anything in this market,"[2] said the boss at Capitol Records. George had managed to get a small company in Chicago, called Vee Jay, to release "Please Please Me" in February of 1963, but the song had flopped. George took "From Me to You" to Capitol records, but they also refused, so he went back to Vee Jay. They released this one too, but the song didn't come close to the top 100, rising to a mere #116—not even a blip on the radar in America.

Still, Brian went to New York. Brian was aware of the challenge that faced him: namely, America regarded anything and everything from another country as a second-rate version of their own. Even if they didn't have it yet, Americans knew they could do it better. American music dominated the UK charts, not the other way around. Not to mention, America already had four young men making music in California: the Beach Boys. Sun-tanned and healthy, clean-cut and confident, the Beach Boys pretty much summed up everything America was about, and therefore, nothing else was needed. Certainly not anything from the United Kingdom.

Still, with his unrelenting confidence in the Beatles, Brian marched right into Capitol Records and asked to speak with their director of eastern operations, Brown Meggs. Capitol had already received three singles from George Martin, but Brian came prepared with a new demo the band had recorded specifically in an attempt to sound more American: "I Want to Hold Your Hand." Brown felt he heard something in the song and agreed to release it—but it was made very clear to Brian that he should not get his hopes up for any kind of positive response. Capitol insisted that America did not want the Beatles. The song was set to be released January 13, 1964, despite Capitol's low expectations.

Next, Brian met with Ed Sullivan, to schedule the band's appearance. While Ed had been impressed by the wit and talent of the Beatles, he was unconvinced that they should appear on his show as anything more than a novelty. Obviously, Ed had not dealt with a manager like Brian Epstein before: What Brian lacked in management experience, he made up for with his tenacious conviction that the Beatles were the best—undoubtedly and absolutely the very best—which resulted in a near-supernatural determination. This time, he was determined to get the band top billing—a spot usually reserved for the best of the best, not some unheard-of act from England; when the meeting was over, the Beatles were booked for not one, but two appearances on *The Ed Sullivan Show,* both at top billing. They were slotted for February 9 and 16 of 1964, one month after their single would be released by Capitol—just enough time to make or break the American Top 100.

That Christmas in the United Kingdom was all about the Beatles. On Christmas day, a televised message from the queen went out to Britain, followed by the Beatles singing "Good King Wenceslas." It had been a very good year. They had given pop music feet to stand on, and boosted a frivolous genre to a mainstream and respectable level. In 1963, they had conquered Britain. In 1964, they would take over America, and then the whole world.

***

In mid-January of 1964, just as their song was released in America, the Beatles did a quick tour to Paris, a few weeks at the Olympia Theater. As it turned out, the French were not very interested in the Beatles: no one recognized them on the streets, and much to their chagrin, the audience at the Olympia was mostly boys. Even more shocking was how bored the audience seemed, clapping along but not screaming or crying, or anything. The show had felt like a failure, but the papers the next day had mostly good reports, except for one that called them has-beens and delinquents.

Good or bad reviews, the Beatles were not reading the papers the next morning, on January 18, 1964. That's because they were informed that "I Want to Hold Your Hand," released just days earlier, had gone straight to number one on the American top 100. Brian and the band sat in silence, and even John had nothing to stay. They were, for once in their lives, completely and utterly speechless. As it sunk in they began jumping around like fools, "We just jumped on each other's backs and screamed the whole place down,"[3] said Paul. They had done it. The Beatles were number one in America.

Capitol Records announced that they had already sold one million copies in the first week—the most ever in their history (at that time, good record sales were around 200,000 copies). The timing was perfect for their spot on *The Ed Sullivan Show,* but even more than that, they had already been booked for Carnegie Hall. As it turned out, a man named Sid Bernstein from American General Artists Corporation had heard the Beatles and their success in Britain and had wanted to bring them to America, right around the time Brian had been in New York. Sid couldn't get a hold of Brian, but he was so confident that the Beatles would do well in New York that he had gone ahead and booked Carnegie Hall anyway—with fingers crossed that he would track down the Beatles in time.

He did. So, in preparation for their American debut, the Beatles had a number one hit (with demands for the entire album pouring in), two nights on *The Ed Sullivan Show* (50,000 people had requested tickets for a studio with 700 seats), and an evening with two performances at the prestigious Carnegie Hall (both show times had already sold out). But even these great accomplishments didn't prepare them for the extent of their reception overseas.

***

Prior to the rise of the Beatles, there was really no such thing as "merchandise" in terms of a band. Occasionally, very popular bands would sell t-shirts at shows, but it was hardly ever for any real profit and more just for a bit of extra publicity. This was true in both the United Kingdom and America. However, Brian began to notice the Beatles' name on a number of items around London and the United Kingdom, such as buttons and shirts. Having high expectations for quality, he attempted to stop productions unless approved, but the task caused him too much stress in the wake of everything else going on.

Brian went to his lawyer, David Jacobs, and asked him to not only find and prosecute people who were stealing the Beatles' name, but also set up an official merchandise operation, with the main goal being to control any American merchandise revenue. David, a busy man, handed the job down to Nicky Byrne, an acquaintance of his with experience in both show business and retailing. Nicky created a company and included five other partners, each with a share of the company. Nicky went to David to approve the partnership with the Beatles, a contract of 90/10; that is, a mere 10 percent of profit to the Beatles. David approved, thinking that profits would be minimal as usual.

Actually, the response to merchandise was quite unusual. Like a virus, Beatles merchandise was popping up literally everywhere, and in every form. There were Beatle wigs copying the mop-top hairstyle, which were being produced at a rate of a few thousand a week. In stores one could find "Beatle Boots," which were black leather shoes with a pointy toe and a small heel, as well as the collarless jackets the band wore (a trend they had picked up from Astrid in Hamburg). But by Christmas of 1963, and in the wake of their new album, merchandise exploded: their faces could be found on belts, blankets, bags, buttons, necklaces, and more, which left Nicky Burns and his partners laughing all the way to the bank.

When "I Want to Hold Your Hand" went to number one in America, Nicky Byrnes was approached by Capitol to sell the rights to the American branch of his merchandise company, Seltaeb (Beatles, spelled backward). Nicky sold the company on two conditions: he got to keep 50 percent, and he received five rare Ferraris for him and his other four investors. Capitol agreed.

Then, after retaining the rights to Seltaeb, and just prior to the Beatles' American tour, Capitol spent $50,000 on publicity—the most the company had ever spent on promotional material. Thousands of radio stations were sent promotional packages, billboards went up, t-shirts and other merchandise were for sale everywhere, and posters, stickers, and flyers appeared all over with a cryptic message: "The Beatles Are Coming."

Nicky, still having some rights to Beatles merchandise, sensed that Capitol was overlooking the actual arrival of the Beatles to kick things off. He took his own initiative and, with the help of a t-shirt maker and two New York radio stations, began announcements on air every 15 minutes: a free t-shirt for every fan that came to welcome the Beatles at the airport.

The band departed Heathrow with 1,000 fans waving them goodbye. The Beatles took up most of the plane, bringing with them Cynthia Lennon (who had finally been publicly recognized as John's wife), Brian, Neil Aspinall, Mal Evans (their other road manager), Dezo Hoffman (their photographer), American record producer Phil Spector, and a plethora of reporters and journalists. As they soared through the air, everyone chatted excitedly about what the tour might be like. They never would have guessed.

As they pulled onto the tarmac, everything seemed normal; that is, until they noticed the 5,000 people waiting behind the glass—a larger turnout than any even a king or queen had ever received. When the doors opened, they thought the roar was just the plane shutting down, when in fact it was that American fans were just twice as loud as British ones. Their publicity manger, Brian Sommerville, had arrived a few days earlier, and he met them on the runway, ushering them inside. With stunned faces, they waved and laughed, shocked by the thousands of screaming girls that lined the roof and windows, pressing their entire bodies against the glass wall.

Brian Sommerville then escorted the band into the main terminal, where a couple hundred journalists awaited them. If any one of them had had doubts about these four young British musicians, they were about to be pleasantly surprised. Despite jet lag and sheer awe at what had just occurred moments before, the Beatles shone with their infamous quick wit:

> "Are those English accents?"
> "It's not English, its Liverpudlian, you see," said George.
> "Liverpool is the . . ." the reporter trailed off.
> ". . . Capital of Ireland," answered Ringo.
> "Is there something you can sing?"
> "No!" replied all of them.
> "We need money first," said John.
> "Are you gonna get a haircut at all?"
> "I had one yesterday," said George, met with much laughter.[4]

By the time the interview was over, nearly every reporter in the room had been impressed by the fast-talking, quick-witted young men.

Their hotel was no better than the airport. They were staying at the Plaza, located on Fifth Avenue, which had to be shut down due to the masses of teenage girls. The Beatles arrived in four Cadillac limos, literally being chased down the street. Hoards of fans pressed against the cars, while the boys each sat inside, waving and laughing in a dazed manner. Paul continually had a radio pressed up to his ear, listening to their every move being documented, and their songs playing back to back, over and over again. It was truly some sort of crazy dream.

They managed to wrestle their way into the Plaza Hotel and checked in, to discover they had been given the entire 12th floor. Brian stayed across town, away from the chaos. The Beatles spent the day in their rooms, alternatively listening to themselves on the radio, and watching themselves on television. Reporters were calling on the phone, and left to their own devices, the band willingly gave interviews and endorsements to any DJ who rang them up—effectively giving away thousands of dollars worth of publicity.

George, who wasn't feeling well, took to bed to try and get better. He awoke the next morning to hear thousands of fans chanting the words to "She Loves You" 12 floors down, despite the drizzling rain. The Beatles discovered the frenzy they could whip up just by leaning out the window—thousands of girls squealing and screaming at the sight of them. It was almost more fun than they could handle—especially when the police arrived to tell them to stop going near the windows. They couldn't help it—they taunted the crowds all day long.

Soon it was time to leave to go perform their first night on *The Ed Sullivan Show*. George was still extremely sick, so Neil stood in for him as they entered the studio. Ed was delighted with the Beatles and excited to have them appear on his show, having discovered that all his intuitions about them were correct. During rehearsal, Brian approached Ed and asked to know the exact wording of Ed's introduction. Ed responded with "get lost."[5] When Ed heard how sick George was—a fever of 104 degrees Fahrenheit—he offered to don a Beatle's wig and stand in for George himself.

When the cameras rolled that night, February 9, America's crime rate was at an all-time low. This was because 60 percent of television-owning Americans were watching *The Ed Sullivan Show*; that is, an estimated 70 million people. George, still very sick, managed to take the stage, knowing it was too big to miss. Americans watched with baited breath as their TVs danced with images of four silly-looking boys, with silly hair and silly accents, singing rock 'n' roll. Hearts across America, hearts that had so recently been broken by the assassination of their beloved president just a few months earlier, were won instantly, and simultaneously.

The next day was a fury of press conferences, back to back, nearly all day long, so much so that the band had to eat during the interviews, unable to even leave the room. No matter how obnoxious, obvious, or ignorant the questions were, they kept up their wits all day.

"Who came up with the name Beatles, and what does it really mean?"

"It means Beatles, doesn't it? But that's just a name, you know, like shoe," replied John.

"We could have been called The Shoes for all you know," added Paul.

"What do you think of American girls?"

American Invasion: The Beatles perform on The Ed Sullivan Show *to a record-breaking 70 million viewers. February 9, 1964. (AP Photo)*

"Marvelous. They're the same as British girls only they've got a different accent," said Paul.

"Is it your ambition to continue what you're doing, or what do you plan to do?"

"Yeah," answered John

"Well, as long as it lasts like this," said Paul, "As long as we keep enjoying it. Once we stop enjoying it, and people stop enjoying it, then uhh. . . ."

"We'll pack in," finished George.[6]

If the band had thought their faces and songs were everywhere before, they were in for a surprise: merchandise had exponentially exploded overnight. Everywhere there were t-shirts, sweatshirts, hats, photos, wigs, pins, buttons, bags, pencils, posters, flags, Beatle dolls, board games, Beatle ice cream, masks, bobbing heads, and more. Brian Epstein was beginning to realize the massive mistake he had made, passing all of this along to David Jacobs, and then to Nicky Byrnes.

At first, when he met up with Nicky in New York, he was pleased to be handed a check for $7,500. "Now how much of this do I owe you?" Brian asked. "Nothing,"[7] replied Nicky, "that's your ten percent." As the comment sunk in, Brian began doing the math in his head. He was furious, and amazed, but soon, just furious. By the end of 1964, an estimated $50 million dollars in merchandise would profit people other than the Beatles.[8]

On February 11, they were met with a blanket of snow over the city and more coming down at an alarming rate. The band was due to depart for Washington, D.C., for their biggest concert to date, held at the Coliseum, which held over 7,000 people. So they took a private train along with their entourage, a few dozen reporters, and a tag-a-long DJ, Murray the K. They were met in Washington by 3,000 teenagers mashed together along the wrought-iron fence at the station, and 7,000 more awaited them at the Coliseum.

The band played on a circular stage, with fans on all sides of them. These fans had read in a magazine that George enjoyed "Jelly Babies," and had come armed to please him by throwing them onstage. What the fans didn't know was that in Britain, Jelly Babies were soft, chewy candies; what they had brought were jelly beans, a much larger, and much harder version. And so as the Beatles played their hits from the stage, they were nailed on all sides with rock-hard jelly beans—as painful as it was dangerous.

The band returned to New York for their two-performance night at Carnegie Hall. While Carnegie Hall has had the best musicians in the world play its stage, the walls had never shaken like they did that night. Girls seemed literally possessed: screaming, shrieking, sobbing, trembling, jumping up and down, pulling their beehived hair, clawing at their eyes and mouths, streams of black eyeliner and mascara running freely down their faces, flinging their arms uncontrollably into the air, wetting their pants, and passing out. John later complained, "It wasn't a rock show; it was just a sort of circus . . . we were like animals."[9]

On February 16 the Beatles made their second appearance on TV, again with Ed Sullivan, though this time it was taped in Miami. And once again, another record was broken: this time an estimated 75 million people tuned in. Shortly after taping the show, the band was given the chance to meet famed boxer Cassius Clay (who would go on to convert to Islam and change his name to Muhammad Ali), who was also in Miami at the time.

Alas, on February 22, the Beatles returned home, exhausted, so exhausted they barely realized that during their absence, London had changed. The stiff-necked, hard-working, drab culture the Brits were known for had vanished. Swinging London had been born. Everything had changed in the city: music, sex, and drugs had taken over. A major reason for this change was a previously unknown drug that caused hallucinations and side effects such as benders lasting several days, orgies, and the desire to wear loose, colorful clothing: it was called LSD.

NOTES

1. Quoted in Philip Norman, *Shout! The Beatles in Their Generation* (New York: Simon & Schuster, 2005), 221.
2. Ibid., 253.
3. Quoted in Keith Badman, *The Beatles: Off the Record* (New York: Music Sales Corp, 2000), 76.
4. Quoted on *The Beatles Ultimate Experience: The Beatles Interview Database,* "Beatles Press Conference: American Arrival 2/7/1964," http://www.beatlesinterviews.org/db1964.0207.beatles.html.
5. Quoted in Peter Brown and Steven Gaines, *The Love You Make: An Insider's Story of The Beatles* (New York: McGraw-Hill Book Company, 1976), 122.
6. Quoted on *The Beatles Ultimate Experience: The Beatles Interview Database,* "Beatles Interview: AP & CBS News, Plaza Hotel 2/10/1964," http://www.beatlesinterviews.org/db1964.0210cbs.beatles.html.
7. Quoted in Norman, *Shout!,* 254.
8. Brown and Gaines, *The Love You Make: An Insider's Story of the Beatles* (New York: McGraw-Hill Book Company, 1976), 129.
9. Quoted in Badman, *The Beatles,* 87.

The budget for the movie was $300,000, a very low budget considering the near guarantee of selling so many albums. The Beatles were offered £25,000, plus part of the profits. The producers had privately decided to go as high as 25 percent, but, once again, Brian Epstein proved a poor businessman, asking for only 7.5 percent. Also, Brian agreed to a three-movie deal, and that all rights would go back to Walter Shenson after 15 years, Brian being unable to imagine that the Beatles might still be famous and profitable that far in the future (in Brian's defense, few musicians had had such long runs of fame at that point in time). It appeared as though, once again, the Beatles would receive very little profit in the long run. *A Hard Day's Night* premiered in July of 1964, grossing $1.3 million dollars the first week alone.

It was supposed to be called *Beatlemania* but was changed at the last minute to a common saying of Ringo's, which he would say after a particularly bad spell of bad-to-back shows, being chased everywhere they went, and popping pills non-stop: *A Hard Day's Night*. The film took place on a train, attempting to portray the hectic life of the Beatles. Ironically, taking six weeks to shoot a film proved to be a near holiday, as they had much time between takes to hang out in their dressing rooms. In true Beatles fashion, the female extras were often escorted to the dressing rooms as well.

This was true for all the girls but one: Pattie Boyd. She had massive blue eyes, colored with thick black eyeliner, a mini-skirt that revealed unending legs, pale skin, and full lips: she was everything they were after. However, being at the top of her game as a model, and now an actress, Pattie was "underwhelmed" by the band's offers to come by their dressing room. She remembers George staring at her the first day of filming, but she had a boyfriend of two years that she was very happy with. First, George asked her to go fool around with him, and he was turned away instantly. So George tried asking her on a proper date, but Pattie also turned that down due to her boyfriend. She also informed George that she was old-fashioned and valued monogamy and faithfulness—code for saying that if she did go out with him, he would have to be with her only, something even John, who was married, and Paul, who genuinely loved Jane, appeared unable to do. She figured this would stop George in his tracks. One can imagine her surprise when George turned up *begging* her for a chance—a Beatle, one of the most famous people on the planet, able to have any girl in the world, begging *her*. Pattie finally accepted, despite her boyfriend of two years, whom she promptly dumped.

The Silver Screen: The Beatles take a break on the set of A Hard Day's Night. *Left: George Harrison's future wife, Pattie Boyd, styles his hair. March 12, 1964. (AP Photo)*

Four weeks later, George bought a house in Esher, and Pattie moved in with him. While they were nuts about each other, Pattie did have some housekeeping to do; that is, on George. Having had women at his beck and call, he seemed to expect Pattie to conform and meet all his desires. Pattie made it very clear she was not that kind of woman, but independent and progressive—a step many women were trying to make in the forward world of Swinging London. It was good for George. Pattie managed to build his self-esteem and work up his self-confidence by having both herself. After all, George had lived permanently in the shadows of John and Paul since he was a teenager. It was Pattie who would inspire him to step out on his own.

Pattie, being so attractive and seeming to have it all, was hated by fans once it became clear that George was taken, despite Brian's best efforts to keep this concealed. Pattie was even threatened by fans, punched and kicked whenever they passed through a crowd.

She wasn't alone, either: Ringo was also off the market. He had an ongoing relationship with a young woman from Liverpool named Maureen Cox, who had been an original Beatle fan at the Cavern. The relationship was on and off, due to Ringo's touring, but when Ringo fell sick with tonsillitis (effectively causing him to miss most of the next tour), it was Maureen who showed up at the hospital to nurse him back to health. They were monogamous from then on, and Maureen was added to the hate list of female Beatle fans around the world. Jane Asher seemed to avoid it only because she was an esteemed actress, and Cynthia was accepted since she had been around from the beginning. Still, all four women lived very public lives and silently shared the bond of knowing their men could, at any moment, be swept away by fame, fortune, or underaged fans.

John also bought a home, and Cynthia was thrilled that she could get out of their prison on the sixth floor, and away from fans. The home John chose was oddly located, some 20 miles away from London, where the action was, and it was an area known for its businessmen, but John felt it was respectable. Cynthia just wanted a home for her and Julian. This home was more than she pictured: located at Weybridge, it was called Kenwood, and it had 24 rooms. Also, it was in desperate need of a renovation. John brought in a renovation team that took over the main areas, forcing Cynthia and Julian up into a small apartment in the top. It would seem that, in many ways, Cynthia was once again stuck in a prison.

In June the Beatles had a hectic tour that covered parts of Europe, Asia, and Australia. This is when Ringo had tonsillitis, so a young chap named Jimmy Nicol drummed for them instead, for most of the tour. The band then went to Sydney, where they had yet another huge wild reception by the fans, followed by more press conferences, which included quips like the following.

> "How did the tickets go in Hong Kong? Did you get full houses there?"
> "I think so," answered John.
> "No. No—a few five quid seats," corrected Paul.
> "I'd see me for five quid," joked John, "wouldn't you?"
> "I wouldn't see you for two-bob, John," replied George.[1]

John's Aunt Mimi had joined them in Hong Kong and followed them to Sydney, but upon arrival in Adelaide, she decided she'd had enough: the sight of 300,000 fans awaiting the band, lining the road all the way from the airport to their hotel in downtown Adelaide, proved too much for her. After seeing 300,000 people waiting for them, the Beatles had yet another press conference:

> "In South Australia, not only teenagers go wild over you, but maybe you noticed today coming in from the airport that a heck of a lot of adults . . . especially grandmas . . ."
> "Yeah," said Paul.
> "I've never seen so many grandmas at once," added John.[2]

That August the Beatles returned to the United States for their first real American tour. They played San Francisco, Las Vegas, Seattle, Vancouver, Los Angeles, Cincinnati, Atlantic City, Philadelphia, Indianapolis, Milwaukee, Chicago, Detroit, Toronto, Montreal, Jacksonville, Baltimore, Boston, New Orleans, Kansas City, Pittsburgh, Denver, Cleveland, Dallas, and New York. They went some 20,000 miles in the air, back and forth across the country, in their private jet: 23 cities, and 25 shows, in just over one month.

If the Beatles had had any hopes of getting to actually see America, they were sorely mistaken. The month was a blur of hotel rooms, limos, planes, and stages. Sometimes they didn't even know what city they were in. And if that was all they saw, for sure almost all they heard was one endless, deafening roar of teenage girls waiting for them around every corner. With them as always were Brian, Neil Aspinall, and Mal Evans, along with Derek Taylor, a publicity manager Brian had hired to replace Brian Sommerville (in truth, Sommerville didn't mind being dumped—he was exhausted!).

Brian was beginning to realize the great mistakes he was making in terms of finances. For example, in Australia, the Beatles were paid a sum that had been agreed upon in 1963, before they had even had a single on the charts. By the time they arrived, they could have been charging 10 times the amount they were receiving, a measly $2,000 per concert. At the time, Brian's stance was that a deal was a deal, and he believed it important to stay true to his word. For the next American tour, Brian swung hard in the other direction, charging between $25,000 and $50,000, plus profits, depending on the size of the venue. Gone were the shady clubs and theaters of Britain, and in came the massive stadiums usually reserved for national teams. While Brian was charging more than any other act in the world, he still demanded that ticket prices be kept low for the sake of the fans.

The American tour opened in San Francisco at the Cow Palace. After the show, so many girls crawled onto their limo that the roof started to cave in, threatening to crush the Beatles. In Seattle, a girl climbed over the stage on a beam and fell, landing at Ringo's feet. In Indianapolis, Ringo disappeared for an entire night, not turning up until literally minutes before their next show, panicking everyone (it turned out he had befriended two cops, who took him to the track where the Indy 500 was raced and let him drive the police car around it all night long). In Los Angeles, the Beatles were forced to line up and shake hands with the Hollywood "in crowd" of actors—in whom they had absolutely no interest.

The Beatles became quite jaded on the tour, fed up with playing songs that no one could hear over the screaming. They took to lip-synching the words, and they played their songs faster than normal in order to get off the stage—and the crowds never noticed. From the moment they went on, the screaming never stopped. They felt like puppets, like robots, playing the same show each night.

As if that was not frustrating enough, endless press conferences with obnoxious reporters asking them again and again about their hair, and an even more endless line-up of "professional groupies" awaited the band in each city they went to. They continued to pop speed pills all day long, just to keep up with the pace. They had never touched hard drugs, and they hardly considered speed a drug since forms of it were available legally, even if they obtained it without a prescription; however, all that was about to change when they were introduced to Bob Dylan.

The Beatles were huge admirers of Bob Dylan and were almost as terrified of him as they were of Elvis. A journalist brought Bob Dylan to their New York hotel room, and Bob, in turn, brought some pot. The four confessed they had never smoked marijuana, which confused Bob, because they had that song about getting high, singing "I get high! I get high!"[3] John sheepishly corrected him that the lyrics were "I can't hide" (from "I Want to Hold Your Hand"). Still, they were intrigued and fascinated with Dylan and agreed to try pot. They attempted to cover the scent by shoving towels under the doors and opening the windows. Dylan kept rolling more joints, and soon enough, everyone in the room, including Brian, was stoned out of their minds. Laughter ensued, and all of them were giggling just from silly looks or even nothing at all. Dylan dug the Beatles, and the Beatles dug Dylan—and his pot.

The reason Bob Dylan was so famous—aside from his enormous contributions to the art of song writing—were his songs of protest. He was famous for his songs of antiwar, propeace, and racial equality. Specifically at that time, race riots were occurring in major cities around the United States as the Beatles toured. Earlier on the tour, in Philadelphia, they had taken the stage to see an audience of over 10,000 faces, all Caucasian. Having taken the stage, it was too late to back down, but the four remained adamant to not let it happen again. When they discovered their concert venue in Florida had separated seating for blacks and whites, they announced they would not play to a segregated crowd: "We've all talked about this and we all agree that we would refuse to play . . . We all feel strongly about civil rights and the segregation issue," said Paul, while John added, "We never play to segregated audiences and we're not going to start now. I'd rather lose our appearance money."[4]

The tour carried on with a now-common hectic pace, new cities nearly every day and a constant roar of girls following them. They were due to have a few days off when the owner of the Kansas City Stadium called and offered them $150,000 to come perform—the most money anyone had ever been paid for an appearance. When they reached Kansas City, they had been on tour nearly a whole month straight, and once again they sat down with the press:

> "John, what does your wife think of all the girls chasing you?"
> "She's not worried. She knows they'll never catch me."
> "Who's the most exciting woman you've ever met?"
> "Ringo's mother is pretty hot!" quipped John.
> "Are you concerned about the poll in Britain which indicates that a group called the Rolling Stones . . ."
> "Wooo!! Wooo!!" the boys hooted in unison.[5]

If questions weren't about their hair, they were usually about the Rolling Stones. The Stones were proving to be the anti-Beatles: shaggier hair, longer and even more unkempt; unmatched dirty clothing; and far more provocative lyrics. The public immediately pitched the Stones against the Beatles, as the Stones climbed the charts in what appeared to be a war of the boys from Britain. To be a "Beatle" meant being the kind of guy a girl could introduce to her parents: clean, polite, and nice; to be a "Stone" was to be a parent's worst nightmare: wild, unruly, and carefree. In reality, the Stones and the Beatles were good friends. At about the time when Brian had turned down the chance to sign the Stones, the Beatles started checking out their shows and were impressed with the sound. The two groups shared quite a lot in common; they were just being marketed differently. They even made sure to release singles at different times, so as not to compete for the number one spot. In fact, the Beatles were jealous of the freedom the Rolling Stones had to wear what they wanted and say whatever they felt like. As the Stones grew to fame with their wild ways, the Beatles felt more and more like Brian's little puppets.

The Beatles returned home from the grueling tour, only to have less than three weeks before starting the next one, around the United Kingdom. They did a five-week tour around Great Britain, due to the outcry of fans who claimed the Beatles had forgotten them for America (especially in Liverpool). On the last night of the tour, at a show in Bristol, a prankster got the better of the Beatles. Someone managed to get up into the ceiling, and with perfect timing during the last chord of "If I Fell," spilled a large bag of flour onto the musicians below. The audience roared as the cloud settled, revealing the Fab Four covered head-to-toe in white powder. After a short pause to take in what had transpired, the Beatles collapsed with laughter, doubled over as if in pain. They managed to pull themselves together to finish the gig and stumbled offstage smiling, for the first time in a long time.

That November the Beatles released a new single, "I Feel Fine" / "She's a Woman." It was yet another Lennon-McCartney song, although this one was more John's. The first few seconds of the song is feedback—a mistake left in the song. Shortly after releasing the song, they took to the studio to record their fourth album in time for Christmas, aptly titled (after their grueling tour in America) *Beatles for Sale,* which included "Eight Days a Week," "Baby's in Black," and a self-abrasive song by John called "I'm A Loser." 1964 had come and gone in a flash.

***

1965 began with a new album, a number one single, and a second movie. It was looking like yet another big year was shaping up. They began filming the movie that spring, which would be called *Help!* In the movie, Ringo accidentally ends up with a special ring that belongs to an East Indian cult, who needs the ring for their ritual human sacrifices. A variety of attempts to get the ring back are foiled, and the Beatles are chased around the world. On set, they seemed happier than before; this is because they had formed a deep relationship with Bob Dylan's marijuana.

In early January, Ringo and Maureen found out Maureen was pregnant. Just weeks later, they were married, on February 11, 1965. "There was [*sic*] no tears," said John, "We'd threatened Mrs. Starkey that if she cried, she wouldn't be one of the gang."[6] At the time of the wedding, Maureen was only 18 years old. Shortly after their small, private, and short wedding, Ringo and the rest of the Beatles had to take off to start filming *Help!*

Much of the film was shot on location in the Bahamas in March of 1965, a nice getaway for the band, at first. However, John insulted the minister of finance when, at a fancy party, John asked him to justify such lavishness when there were children and elderly folks starving and abandoned on the island (which John had seen for himself). The day after the party, they were asked to leave the Bahamas.

The next shooting location was Austria. One day the Beatles stepped out onto their balcony to see tens of thousands of Austrians gathered on the streets, chanting for them. They immediately grabbed their little black combs and placed them over their lips. They stepped back onto the porch and pretended to have Hitler moustaches, while throwing their other arm up into the air. Given Austria's history, one might imagine they were about to be kicked out of another country. On the contrary, the crowd roared with laughter.

Back in England, the Beatles were still on the outside of the Swinging London phenomenon, but not for long. One night, George and Pattie and John and Cynthia went to a dinner party their dentist was throwing (straight teeth were becoming all the rage in Britain at the time). This dentist had worked on all four Beatles and seemed to be quite a nice fellow, though he did seem to have that "Swinging 60s" vibe to him. After dinner, the dentist popped some sugar cubes into some coffees and made everyone drink. Afterward, he announced they had all just taken LSD.

George and John were furious; Pattie and Cynthia were terrified. The four of them left immediately, unaware of the effects of LSD. George managed to get them downtown to a nightclub, attempting to lose the dentist, who was following them. They got into the elevator and saw a red light, which, in their minds, turned into fire. The elevator opened into the club with the four of them screaming and hysterical. Then they left and attempted to get to George's house. George was unable to drive above a snail's pace; Cynthia was trying to make herself sick, in order to throw up the drug; John couldn't stop talking, words just spilling from his mouth nonstop; Pattie had a strange urge to smash windows. They managed to get home, terrified. "It was a horrifying experience that I will never forget," said Cynthia, "an *Alice in Wonderland* experience." John seemed less affronted, saying "it was terrifying, but it was fantastic."[7]

That April, the band recorded their next hit, "Ticket to Ride" / "Yes It Is." It was cowritten, of course, by John and Paul, but with better harmonies and more original lyrics than their previous songs. Instead of straightforward messages like "She Loves You" and "I Want to Hold Your Hand," "Ticket to Ride" was a metaphor for an ending relationship. That was a turning point, lyrically, for the two composers, toward slightly more cryptic messages in their songs. In addition, Abbey Road had updated its recording equipment, and within the house that the main studio was in there was also Studio Two, which was now pretty much exclusively for Beatles use whenever they wished.

In July the Beatles released "Help!," the title song of their new movie, as a single, and it went straight to number one. The soundtrack to the movie, also called *Help!*, was released in August of 1965, and also went to number one almost instantly. The soundtrack was the Beatles fifth album and included a song written by John called "You've Got to Hide Your Love Away," which was obviously influenced by John's new obsession with Bob Dylan. There was also the very first solo song, written and sung by Paul alone. Originally titled "Scrambled Eggs," it was now called "Yesterday." The song has gone on to be covered over 3,000 times by other musicians (a Guiness World Record), and is considered one of Paul's very best works. Finally, the actual movie, *Help!*, was released August 23.

Right before the movie came out, the Beatles went back to America for another short tour. On August 15, they played Shea Stadium in New York, to the largest crowd ever at the time: an estimated 56,000 people. "It was marvellous," said John, "I think it was the biggest live show that anyone has ever done and it was fantastic, you know!" They walked away with $100,000 as per their contract, and $60,000 in extra profits, their biggest paycheck to date.

The tour went on to include Toronto, Atlanta, Houston, Chicago, Minneapolis, Los Angeles, San Diego, and San Francisco. They played a city each night for six nights, until they arrived in Los Angeles, where they were rewarded with almost a whole week off to relax in Beverly Hills. Of course, the fans found out almost immediately. Crowds of people stood outside the property where they were day and night, as usual, so the band was confined to their mansion for most of their stay. This was all right by them, so long as they got to rest. Since they couldn't go out, they had people visit them, such as the up-and-coming folk-rock band the Byrds, along with Peter Fonda. The Byrds brought the Beatles a welcome gift: LSD. John and George's second time around proved less frightening than the first, and it seemed that acid would be the new drug of the Beatles.

Also during their time in Los Angeles, the Beatles finally found the courage to go meet their idol, Elvis, something they had been

Stadium Mayhem: The Beatles play at Shea Stadium in New York to a record-breaking audience of about 50,000. August 23, 1965. (AP Photo)

putting off since their first tour. They arrived at his home in Bel Air, and the house was surrounded with police to ensure their safety. At first, the musicians were stunned into silence. "Well if we're just going to sit here looking at each other all night, I'm going to bed,"[8] remarked Elvis. Once the tension subsided a little, with the aid of scotch whiskey, the Beatles and Elvis jammed and talked about what life on the road as a superstar is like. If anyone could understand their predicament, it was Elvis. Still, it had been a long time since Elvis had had a number one hit, or drawn crowds of the magnitude that the Beatles did. There was also a nervousness that penetrated the overall mood of the meeting, making it almost impossible to get comfortable. One would think that a meeting of two such history-makers would be amazing, but it proved to be an awkward disappointment. The students had surpassed their master.

In October, the Beatles received the Member of the British Empire, or MBE. MBE is the lowest rank in the Order of Chivalry, an award that is usually given to war heroes, philanthropists, authors, and others along those lines. For the Beatles, a rock 'n' roll band, to receive it was a major honor. But they seemed unimpressed with the induction, and a few older inductees were equally unimpressed, to the point of returning their MBEs in protest. They might have had reason to do so, considering that "The Beatles smoked marijuana in the lavatories at Buckingham Palace while waiting to receive the MBE,"[9] according to John.

The Beatles released their sixth album, *Rubber Soul,* that December. The album went to number one, but for only seven weeks. It was much darker and moodier than earlier albums, with songs like "Norwegian Wood," which featured George on the sitar—an instrument he had been inspired to learn during the filming of *Help!,* which featured East Indian actors, and mystic Eastern music. Also on this album was "Girl," a song with a dark, brooding undertone, about a sort of dream girl who keeps a boy coming back to her even though she's bad for him. In the chorus, there's a long sucking sound, like inhaling through one's teeth, possibly to mimic inhaling marijuana.

Looking back, *Rubber Soul* was a real turning point for the Beatles, as it was the first album into which they invested much time and thought. They were moving away from simple pop songs and gravitating toward something that could really be called art. Unlike their 13-hour binge recording sessions of the past, this album came over a period of weeks and spiraled deeper as the recording went on. It included a song by John that would go on to be considered near genius by critics, called "In My Life," as well as a catchy, but smart, love song by Paul, called "Michelle." Of course, one might also consider that this was the first album that was directly influenced not only by their newfound love, marijuana, but also by their increasing experiments with LSD. Although *Rubber Soul* eventually gained recognition as an excellent album, it was met at the time with much criticism for not being like their other works.

Immediately after releasing the album, the Beatles put out a single, "We Can Work It Out" / "Day-Tripper." Following that, they did a U.K. winter tour. On this tour they played what would be their last performance in Liverpool. It would have also been their last chance to go back to the Cavern Club, but during this time Ray McFall, the owner, was forced to shut the club down due to bankruptcy. The year came to a close with three albums, three tours, an MBE, another movie, a meeting with Elvis, and Ringo welcoming his first child, Zak, into the world. To top it all off, George proposed to Pattie at Christmas.

George and Pattie got married just one month later, on January 21, 1966. This left Paul as the only unmarried Beatle. John and Ringo had the ideal wives, who didn't mind staying home, raising kids, and being alone; that is, their wives in no way impeded upon their success or fame. Of course, the difference was that John was scornful of Cynthia and treated her as beneath him, as a mistake from his childhood, whereas Ringo truly loved Maureen, and the two were endlessly happy. George loved Pattie and embraced her as an independent and intelligent woman, a far cry from his original attempts to make her conform. While Pattie had mild fame as a model and actress, it was only Paul who had to deal with a famous girlfriend. Jane had quite the resume and had no desire to give it up and settle down as Paul wanted her to. Their relationship was at a standstill, but they continued seeing each other anyway.

The Beatles set to work on their next album in April, which would be titled *Revolver*. *Revolver* marked their passage from pot to acid as their drug of choice, most notably seen in their experiments with instruments and sound. The album included an unheard-of three songs by George, including "Taxman," which enjoyed some success as a single. It included "Here, There and Everywhere" by Paul, about Jane, and "Tomorrow Never Knows," written by John on acid while reading the *Tibetan Book of the Dead*. The strangest song was, of course, "Yellow Submarine," which Paul had penned late one night, as a joke. The most popular song of the whole album was "Eleanor Rigby," another song by Paul, which would go on to much long-term success. All in all, *Revolver* was the Beatles, united. They played in such harmony; they played *together*. In the years to come, this togetherness would be lost.

NOTES

1. Quoted on *The Beatles Ultimate Experience: The Beatles Interview Database*, "Beatles Press Conference: Sydney Australia 6/11/1964," http://www.beatlesinterviews.org/db1964.0611.beatles.html.
2. Quoted on *The Beatles Ultimate Experience: The Beatles Interview Database*, "Beatles Press Conference: Adelaide, Australia 6/12/1964," http://www.beatlesinterviews.org/db1964.0612.beatles.html.
3. Quoted in Philip Norman, *John Lennon: The Life* (New York: Doubleday Canada, 2008), 375.
4. Quoted in Keith Badman, *The Beatles: Off The Record* (New York: Music Sales Corp, 2000), 124–25.
5. Quoted on *The Beatles Ultimate Experience: The Beatles Interview Database*, "Beatles Press Conference: Kansas City 9/17/1964," http://www.beatlesinterviews.org/db1964.0917.beatles.html.
6. Quoted in Badman, *The Beatles*, 139.
7. Ibid., 146–47.
8. Quoted in Peter Brown and Steven Gaines, *The Love You Make: An Insider's Story of the Beatles* (New York: McGraw-Hill, 1976), 189.
9. Quoted in Badman, *The Beatles*, 184.

CHAPTER EIGHT

Things Fall Apart

They were suddenly called Fred and His Incredible Shrinking Grateful Airplanes.

John Lennon

Before their American tour, the Beatles took off on a world tour that would have a few threatening incidents of its own. They started in their old stomping grounds, Hamburg, but the nostalgia was limited, since Hamburg had changed considerably: their old pubs were gone, and venues closed, replaced by more strip clubs or left empty. The thrill of the Reeperbahm had vanished. They managed to meet up with old friends, including Astrid, who still kept a candle burning in her room 24 hours a day, under a large eerie photo of Stu Sutcliffe.

Next was Tokyo. They arrived to discover that a protest group against Western influences on Japan had made threats on the Beatles' lives—in fact, they'd vowed the Beatles would not leave Japan alive. The band was rushed to their hotel and confined to the top floor while a small army stood guard outside, and on the floor below. The Beatles played three shows and were surprised by the polite crowd, who sat in their seats and clapped after each song; it was the first time they had been able to hear themselves play in a while.

The Beatles left Japan alive, but they came across more hard times in the Philippines, where they were lucky to escape unscathed. The president's wife had planned a party for herself and 300 lucky children to meet the Beatles. A formal invitation had been extended, but it was received by Tony Barrow, the Beatles publicity manager, who never responded to it. So when Brian was informed early one morning that the Beatles were expected at lunch, he turned down the offer. The band had an agreement to not attend government functions after a disaster at the British Embassy in Washington on their first tour, where stiff old men of high social status mocked the intelligence, style, and social standing of the Beatles. The band had been humiliated and degraded, and Brian had promised they would never have to go through it again. They had no idea they had turned down such an important invitation and played their two sets that afternoon to 100,000 fans, with no issues.

It was Brian who noticed the evening news broadcast, which stated that the Beatles had never showed up for their party. Not only had they offended the president and his wife, but to make matters worse, the 300 children that had been invited were orphans, cripples, and victims of war. Brian had still not clued the band in to what had happened, and they went to bed as usual. When they awoke, they were confused to find their hotel almost empty of staff, with not even a cook to make breakfast. It was Mal who found a local paper that read "Beatles Snub President."

They turned on the TV to discover it was all over the news. They decided to head for the airport that minute and attempt to leave as fast as possible. They had to load their own equipment and find a driver willing to take them to the airport, where a flight was waiting for them. With no police to escort them, they had to battle morning traffic by themselves, only to arrive at the airport to a crowd of hundreds of angry Filipinos who simultaneously kicked, punched, and pushed the Beatles. After being meticulously screened at the gate, with the angry mob standing just outside the windows, screaming for justice, they got on the plane.

On the plane to London, they told Brian that they wouldn't do another tour. They knew that they made more than enough money from their albums alone, and they had been touring for nearly four years. They were exhausted, overworked, and tired of playing to crowds that didn't listen but just screamed. Brian was so worry-stricken over this news that he broke out in hives all over his body and spent a month in bed. A month after their arrival home, on August 5, 1966,

Revolver was released along with a single, "Paperback Writer" / "Eleanor Rigby."

Even though they had sworn off touring, the Beatles still had to honor the shows they had agreed to do in America, which appeared to be in great jeopardy. Months earlier, in April of 1966, John had given an interview published in the *London Evening Standard* by a writer the Beatles knew well, named Maureen Cleave. A progressive writer, she asked John about his thoughts on religion, to which John gave a response that caused a backlash he never imagined: "Christianity will go. It will vanish and sink. I needn't argue about that. I'm right and will be right. We're more popular than Jesus now."[1] At the time, there was little to no backlash about this comment in England, or Europe, where religious zealots were few; however, in July, when excerpts were reprinted in a teen magazine called *Datebook,* a fury burned across America like a wildfire.

Churches, especially in the "Bible Belt" of the southern states, held book-burning rallies, where teenagers were encouraged to bring any and all Beatle paraphernalia to dump into the fire. Record stores sent back albums and refused to have any Beatles' music in stock, while more than 35 radio stations stopped playing Beatles music altogether. Even the Ku Klux Klan (KKK) was offended and nailed Beatles albums to crosses set on fire, as well as making threatening remarks about the Beatles' safety if they returned to America, which they were due to do in August.

Brian urged John to apologize, or at least clarify what he meant, and John begrudgingly agreed and did so at an impromptu press conference held in Chicago. At first, John was only willing to say that he had been misinterpreted, "I'm not anti-God, anti-Christ, or anti-religion. I was not saying that we are greater or better," desperately trying to reword his opinion, since he didn't believe he was wrong so much as misunderstood. Still, it was not good enough. The reporters pressed him to actually apologize, and John caved in, saying "I still don't know quite what I've done . . . but if it will make you happy, then okay, I'm sorry."[2]

Of course, John was not sorry, not in the sense that the public wanted. He was sorry to have offended people, but he did not want to take back what he had said. Many more interviews about the subject followed, but John was fed up with explaining himself. The Beatles continued on their American tour, complete with KKK picketers and an overwhelming fear of being killed each time they took the stage. The tour came and went, but it could not have ended fast enough for

Farewell: The Beatles depart London for their American tour, despite the riots against John Lennon's infamous Jesus quote. It would be their last tour as a band. August 11, 1966. (AP Photo/Harris)

four young men who just wanted to go home. It was no longer fun. The tour finished at Candlestick Park in San Francisco—and it would be their last live show, ever.

Arriving home, they took much-needed time apart, for the first time in years. In September, John took off for Germany, where he had accepted a role in a movie. He was to play Private Gripeweed in *How I Won the War*, directed by Richard Lester. At approximately 7:30 A.M., on September 6, 1966, John's long and tousled hair for which he was so incredibly famous was cut short to an army-style crew cut. The hair was burned immediately to avoid it being sold to fans. Also during the film his character wore round, wire eyeglasses, in the style of the 1920s, a style he would grow to like, and keep. Images of John with short hair made front page news around the world.

When John returned to London, many opportunities awaited him. He was bored with acting, and it was art that became his next passion. He went to an opening at the Indica Gallery on November 9, having heard that the artist was very progressive. The gallery's owner sent the artist over to John to introduce herself. She was tiny and Japanese, dressed all in black, with a mass of black hair. She handed John a piece of paper that said "Breathe." Her name was Yoko Ono.

John was put off by the seriousness of the gallery, so he looked at Yoko and said "Like this?" and let out a heavy pant. Yoko replied "that's it."[3] Yoko's exhibit was full of pieces that John found both ridiculous and alluring. There was an apple on a stand selling for £200, a plank of wood with rusty bent nails, and his favorite, a ladder up to the ceiling, where a tiny card read a word that would possibly alter his life forever: *Yes.* Both John and Yoko felt a strange connection as they talked. He had officially met the woman who would ruin his marriage, break up his band, bear his child, and change the course of his life completely.

Brian, unfortunately, was lost without John and the Beatles. His coworkers assured him that there was much to be done, even without touring, but Brian found no solace in that. He felt unneeded, unwanted, and unnecessary. He spiraled into an agonizing depression and began taking far too many drugs, including LSD. The year came to an end with the Beatles back at Abbey Road attempting to make a new album that would end up changing the face of a generation. While the Beatles were looking ahead, Brian was falling behind. He knew that the Beatles had become too big for him, that he had made too many mistakes as their manager, and that the four people who brought him his only sense of joy would soon realize they would be better off without him.

****

1967 was the start of the reign of the hippy. The heart of the movement was in San Francisco, in areas such as the Haight-Ashbury neighborhood, where communities of hippies roamed free, barefoot and stoned, and an onslaught of American youth made a pilgrimage to join the ranks, in protest against America's intervention in Vietnam and a war that no one had asked America to be involved in. For the first time in history, the war was broadcast on TV, and suddenly it was clear to many people that, as unbelievable as it was, America was no longer the good guy.

Up until this point, Americans had been safe and secure in knowing that their country was good; in fact, it was the greatest country on Earth. And up until recently, music in America reflected just that: poppy, happy songs about surfing, falling in love, and the great

American way of life. American music had been proud music, music that boasted of its love for its country. America was the proud, the good, the superhero of the world; that is, until images and reports from Vietnam began to tell a different story, a story of arrogance, greed, and injustice.

In February of 1967, the Beatles released their next single, which was "Strawberry Fields Forever" / "Penny Lane." It was their first single that did not make it to number one, blocked by "Please Release Me" by Engelbert Humperdink. Still, the album marked the transition the Beatles had begun to make on *Revolver*; that is, the transition to psychedelic music. "Penny Lane" was written completely by Paul and represented a real place: a bus roundabout in Liverpool. "Strawberry Fields Forever" was written completely by John and was also about a real place: a boys' reformatory near where John grew up.

Revolver continued to do well as an album. Though music critics didn't realize what a masterpiece it was at the time, other musicians loved and responded to it, musically. A whole slew of albums started coming out, with the same sense of connected songs and wholeness. One of these albums was, surprisingly, by the Beach Boys, called *Pet Sounds*. Paul himself said it was a perfect album and wasn't sure how he could counter it. Inspired, the Beatles returned to Abbey Road Studios and began the recording sessions that would be their response to *Pet Sounds*. The album would eventually be called *Sgt. Pepper's Lonely Hearts Club Band*.

There were 12 songs on the album, each of which was a piece of art that could stand alone. The music was sheer genius—so much so that Brian Wilson of the Beach Boys, who had recorded *Pet Sounds*, actually gave up working on his new album, he was so sure that *Sgt. Pepper* could not be topped. The Beatles' new album was released in June of 1967 and rocketed to number one: *Sgt. Pepper* would go on to define a generation. It set the backdrop to the protests, the sexual freedom revolution, and the antiwar and propeace movement, and it perfectly personified the forthcoming "Summer of Love."

The album had the title track "Sgt. Pepper's Lonely Hearts Club Band," written by Paul. It began with the realization that band names like "The Beatles" and "The Monkees" or "Gerry and the Pace Makers" were going out of style, and instead bands were calling themselves long, complicated names. In John's words, "They were suddenly called Fred and His Incredible Shrinking Grateful Airplanes."[4] So Paul came up with the idea of parodying the Beatles as somebody else, and *Sgt. Pepper* and his band was born.

There was a song written for Ringo called "With A Little Help from My Friends," which was a sing-along–styled song, although it was later banned on some radio stations for the line "I get high with a little help from my friends"—which John and Paul said was "spiritually" high, like elation or joy, not drugs. Of course, this argument did not work for John's other song, "Lucy in the Sky with Diamonds." John stressed that the song was about his son's friend Lucy, of whom Julian had drawn a picture, depicting her flying in the sky among the stars, or "diamonds." As touching as the story was, it didn't help that the song was not only full of hallucinogenic images, in a sort of "Alice in Wonderland" theme, but that the title, when abbreviated, was LSD. Even though John was doing LSD almost daily at the time, he remained adamant that that was not the message of the song.

Among other drug references was the song "I'm Fixing a Hole," which was said to be about a heroin addict; as well, "For the Benefit of Mr. Kite," which sang of "Henry the Horse," was said to be a code-word for heroin, although John said he took the name from an antique circus poster. Then there was "A Day in the Life," whose lyrics spoke of "4,000 holes" in a road—literally, the roads in Blackburn, Lancashire—but it was taken to be figurative for a heroin addict's arm. The song also stood out for its highly suggestive lyric, which surpassed all other cheeky references at the time and got the song banned on many radio stations: "I'd love to turn you on!" They also brought in a 42-piece orchestra and instructed the musicians to play without a score—their only instructions were to play between the lowest and highest notes in the key given. After a massive orchestral climax, the song ended with a note of 20,000 Hertz, audible only to dogs.

Almost as momentous was the album's cover. It featured the Beatles in brightly colored band uniforms (pink, blue, yellow, and scarlet), holding up various instruments. Surrounding them were the faces of their heroes and influences: Bob Dylan, Marlon Brando, Oscar Wilde, William Burroughs, Karl Marx, Edgar Allan Poe, Aldous Huxley, Marilyn Monroe, Shirley Temple, Buddha, several Indian gurus, and even Stu Sutcliffe, among many more. The band's name was spelled out in flowers before them, and then many random images and inside jokes were scattered around, such as a doll with a shirt reading "Welcome The Rolling Stones."

The BBC then invited the Beatles to perform on their new program, titled *Our World*, which would be broadcast via satellite around the world (the newest technological advance). John and Paul wrote a song just for the event and in perfect time for the Summer of Love, which had just begun. The band wore psychedelic outfits in wild colors and invited their good friends the Rolling Stones and Eric Clapton, among other musicians, to join them. Performed live, and accompanied by a 13-piece orchestra, the song was "All You Need Is Love," and it was seen and heard in 31 countries and watched by a global audience of more than 500 million people.

While the Beatles' new album was thriving, Brian was not. Depressed by his "loss" of the Beatles, he took to gobbling up drugs and growing his hair long (in a last attempt to become a Beatle himself, perhaps). He took so many drugs that he would often be up for several days at a time on uppers, and then crash into bed for several more, having taken too many downers.

All You Need: The Beatles pose for a photo during a rehearsal for the broadcast of "All You Need Is Love" at EMI Studios. It would be the first international broadcast ever and would be watched by over 300 million people in 24 different countries. June 24, 1967. (AP Photo)

The Beatles invited Brian to come on a trip with them that they were taking to Wales. They were going to spend 10 days studying under a Buddhist holy man who taught Transcendental Meditation, a man named Maharishi Mahesh Yogi. It was George and Pattie who had first brought the rest of the Beatles and their wives to hear the Maharishi speak, and they were instantly sold. They signed up for the 10-day trip and prepared to leave the very next day. Brian declined, saying he had plans for the long weekend, but that he might try to visit them afterward.

On August 25, 1967, the Beatles and their wives opted to travel via public train, something they had not done in many years. A massive crowd of reporters and fans had gathered, and the Beatles had to push through on their own, along with Mick Jagger, of the Rolling Stones, and Marianne Faithful, his girlfriend. As they boarded the train, John realized Cynthia wasn't with them. Cynthia had been stopped by guards who thought she was a fan, and although she chased the train, she soon gave up and burst into tears. Much like their relationship, John took off and left Cynthia behind. "I was crying because the incident seemed symbolic of what was happening to my marriage," she said later. "I felt certain that the loneliness I was experiencing on that platform would become permanent one day."[5]

While Cynthia arranged other transportation, the rest of the group arrived in Bangor, Wales, after a tight ride in a private compartment. They were buzzing and excited about their 10 days, eager to experience something new, even though they had heard that the Maharishi was wanted in India for financial issues and inappropriate sexual behavior. They dismissed this as all rumor when they sat down with the giggly, bubbly, happy man. The Maharishi promised inner peace, tranquility, and sublime consciousness that surpassed any drug-induced experience.

After one day at the meditation retreat, the Beatles announced they were giving up drugs, even John. They announced they had discovered that drugs hindered spiritual harmony, and that meditation achieved the same feelings of elation and ecstasy that any drugs did. They were on top of the world, with new visions for their lives and their music, full of the sensation that they had finally discovered something real. They felt more alive than they had in years. Unfortunately, back in London, the same was not true for Brian.

Brian was found dead in his bedroom that Sunday. The last time he had been seen was Friday night, when he had dinner with Peter Brown and Geoffrey Ellis—both partners from NEMS. During the dinner, Brian had taken off to go to London suddenly (in pursuit of a different type of male company), though he did return that night. However, by Sunday morning the house staff was very worried, having not seen or heard from Brian nearly the whole weekend—he had not left his room once since he had returned.

The staff began phoning Brian's closest acquaintances, such as Peter Brown, and when a few of them arrived, as well as a doctor, they went to Brian's room together. They knocked and buzzed to no answer, and finally the doctor knocked the door down. Brian lay across his bed in a mess of papers, documents, and other business work. Brian Epstein was dead.

Everyone assumed it was suicide, but it was not. An autopsy report showed that it was, indeed, an overdose of Cabitrol, the drug Brian used to sleep. But it was a gradual overdose, not just one night, but over a few days. Still, it is easy to see why the rumors of suicide spread: Brian had attempted to overdose himself on a few other occasions, and many times by accident. He was homosexual, which, to many people in 1967, was reason enough to want to end it all. As well, the Beatles appeared to be abandoning him, not to mention that less than a month before, in an interview with *The Melody Maker*, Brian had admitted to doing LSD and had been receiving much backlash. Also in that interview he was asked what he was most afraid of. Brian eerily responded, "Loneliness. I hope I'll never be lonely, although, actually, one inflicts loneliness on one's self to a certain extent."[6]

In Bangor, Wales, the Beatles were busy focusing on themselves. Peter Brown, who had been there when they found Brian, was the one who phoned Paul to inform him. Paul was shocked silent. He ran and told the others. They were equally stunned. They immediately went to see the Maharishi, who told them that death was insignificant, that Brian had moved on to the spiritual world, and that they should usher him on with laughter and good thoughts. With this thought, they attempted to be happy, so that Brian would receive their good karma, though the press reporters were baffled by four smiling Beatles. Of course, the sadness crept through, and each of them mourned privately upon returning to London. John was especially wounded, having once again lost someone he loved, having once again been abandoned.

Since it was not a suicide, Brian's affairs were not in order. In Brian's will, he stipulated that his brother, Clive, take over all his assets, including NEMS, but unfortunately for Clive, NEMS was in the middle of changing hands. Brian had been in the middle of trying to sell the business, except for the Beatles, to an Australian businessman, Robert Stigwood. Clive met with the Beatles to inform them that Stigwood still planned to buy NEMS, but that he was arguing that the contract had included the Beatles. The Beatles threw a legal fit, and Stigwood gave in, although he did depart with a hefty sum: £25,000, and half of the NEMS music lineup, including the Bee Gees, Jimi Hendrix, and Cream. But the Beatles were safe; Clive had a hold on NEMS and was starting an expansion company called Nemporer, and Peter Brown took over in Brian's place, temporarily, until the matter of a manager could be decided.

On September 2, the Beatles and Peter Brown met to discuss Paul's new idea. Earlier that year, in April, Paul had gone to America to see Jane on her birthday, where she was on tour with a play. While there, Paul went to San Francisco. While George had once been appalled by the Haight-Ashbury district, Paul was taken by it. Flying home, he did a lot of thinking about the free-loving nomadic life of the San Francisco hippies, as well as Ken Kesey's Merry Pranksters, about whom he had recently heard. They were a group of American hippies who traveled around in a bus, drinking acid-infused Kool-Aid (summed up in Tom Wolfe's book, *The Electric Kool-Aid Acid Test*). All this came to the surface as Paul revealed his new idea: a tour. And not just any tour: the *Magical Mystery Tour*.

Paul already had the title song done, and he wanted to make an album and a movie for television. The movie would feature the Beatles and an entourage driving around the United Kingdom on a magical bus. While Paul was confident about making a movie, the rest of the band was uneasy. None of them know how to produce a film, let alone write a script. But on September 11, with no manager to tell them right from wrong, they embarked to film what would be the first major Beatle disaster.

The *Magical Mystery Tour* was not the groovy experience Paul was hoping for. They piled onto a 60-seat bus that was covered in signs announcing it as the Magical Mystery Tour. Along with the Beatles, there was a plethora of people they picked to join them, including dwarfs, fat ladies, journalists, and friends. They expected the trip of their lives, but all they got was traffic, and more traffic. The scenes they filmed were random, unordered, and confusing. Once they returned home, the footage went to editing, where the Beatles would randomly drop in and have their say on how it should be put together. The footage was edited, and reedited, over and over again.

The movie aired on December 26, 1967, with 15 million people watching, on BBC. The reviews were less than desirable, with most newspapers dismissing the film as a complete waste of time. Despite the backlash, the movie did well in terms of viewers. The video, when released, grossed $2 million in rentals, and the companion album still sold $8 million within its first two weeks. If it was not obvious yet, it was now: Beatles fans were die-hard fans to the end, no matter what the band got into. Sales of the Christmas release did well too—they had released "Hello, Goodbye" / "I Am the Walrus" in November and it was number one by December in both the United Kingdom and America.

The movie had cost them £40,000. Brian's overly cautious voice was gone, leaving the Beatles to make their own decisions for the first time since 1962. As it turned out, while on paper they appeared to be millionaires, the truth was that the Beatles were broke. This was due to a number of factors: first, the moment they became famous and starting selling albums, they were forced into a staggering 94 percent tax bracket, meaning they got to keep 6 percent of their earnings, after Brian's cut; second, they were still on a royalty rate with EMI of one penny per album, which they had agreed to back in 1963; third, they had missed out on the merchandise profits; fourth, their first few tours had been for barely enough to cover travel costs. For years they had been living off of Brian's "brown bags," a loophole Brian had found that involved concert venues agreeing to pay him in cash. Without the brown bags, there was very little money left for the band, though they had been spending regardless, on houses, cars, clothes, travel, and frivolous musical efforts, like the *Magical Mystery Tour.*

While Brian's brown bags were gone, he had had one idea that outlived him. He had come up with an idea to turn the Beatles into some kind of corporation, allowing them to invest in themselves and have creative control over every aspect of their music. More than that, they could even open Beatles stores around the world, selling merchandise and reaping the profits. All of this would allow for tax cuts, writing off flops, creative breathing room, and more money—it seemed like a perfect idea.

So it was put into play almost immediately. The Beatles were excited about the idea of playing businessmen and were determined to show the world that young people, hippies, and rock stars could do business as well as, if not better than, stuffy old men. In April of 1967, the four partnered into Beatles & Co. and started dreaming up various branches they could open. Through the summer they met some people who would chart a course to financial disaster, four of them being a design collective called the Fool. The Fool, comprising three Dutch hippies, was hired to dress the Beatles for "All You Need Is Love." It was successful, so they were then given £100,000 in September 1967 to open a Beatle boutique and stock it with their bohemian designs. Their collective idea was a hippy's paradise, a sort of Garden of Eden, so the boutique was called, quite simply, Apple.

The boutique opened on December 7, 1967. Only John and George attended, as Ringo was off filming a part for the movie *Candy*, and Paul had taken a trip to a farm he had purchased in Scotland, called High Park. The shop was on the corner of Paddington and Baker Streets, and the side of the building was painted in wild psychedelic images. The main floor was the boutique, selling trinkets, incense, and brightly colored, loose-fitting clothing. The top floor was the offices, for the various other Apple businesses they were forming: Apple Publishing, being run by Terry Doran; Apple Records, run by Ron Kass and managed by Mal Evans; Apple Films, run by Dennis O'Dell; a talent department, run by Peter Asher (Jane Asher's brother); and Apple Retail, the boutique, being run by none other than John's boyhood friend, Pete Shotton. Pete was running the boutique with one main objective: spend money before it got taken by "the taxman."

1967 ended with the flop of the *Magical Mystery Tour*, but 1968 seemed bright, as the four were like children in a toy store, with money at their whim to spend on their own company. They changed the name of the company to Apple Corps Ltd., a pun of Paul's, and made Neil Aspinall the managing director, and Alistair Taylor, from NEMS, the general manager. They also brought in Peter Brown from NEMS to be part of their board of directors, and Brian Lewis to be their lawyer. The goal of Apple Corps was to be fun, to be young and free, and to be the antibusiness. Their doors, and their pockets, were open to pretty much anything.

NOTES

1. Quoted in Maureen Cleave, "How Does a Beatle Live? John Lennon Lives Like This." *The London Evening Standard*, April 4, 1966.
2. Quoted on *The Beatles Ultimate Experience: The Beatles Interview Database*, "Beatles Press Conference: Chicago 8/12/1966," http://www.beatlesinterviews.org/db1966.0812.beatles.html.

CHAPTER NINE

A Heavy Yoko To Bear

Oh. Hi.

Yoko Ono

Enjoying the lifestyle that accompanied being open to anything, the Beatles decided to go to India to study under the Maharishi. It was, of course, mostly George and Pattie's idea, and they managed to wrangle in the rest of the Beatles and their ladies, Pattie's sister Jenny, Mal Evans, a singer called Donovan, Mike Love of the Beach Boys, and an actress named Mia Farrow. They left on February 16, 1968, flying to Delhi, then taking taxis, and then finally walking the dirt road up to the ashram.

The group wore traditional Indian clothes and spent the days in meditation and listening to the Maharishi talk. The four would compete for the longest meditation and grew out their beards and moustaches. At night, they would sit under the stars and write songs together, without drugs or booze, and the women would talk in their rooms, usually about life as the partner of a Beatle. Cynthia took up painting and drawing, which she had hardly done since she had met John at Liverpool Art College so long ago. John became stronger and healthier without drugs and spent hours in meditation each day. Cynthia found hope for their marriage during their time at the ashram; ironically, John was writing letters to Yoko Ono nearly every day.

Ringo and Maureen left after only 10 days, as Maureen could not stand the flies, and they missed their children. The next to leave were Paul and Jane, after nine weeks, secretly feeling that they were far too mature and sophisticated to take part in such mystical things. As they left, another man came to stay: Alex Mardas, a Greek-turned-Londoner who had befriended John via Mick Jagger. The Beatles had met Alex in the summer, around the same time they met the Fool. Alex claimed to be an inventor of amazing new technologies that would interest and supposedly benefit the Beatles and would revolutionize their music and company. John nicknamed him Magic Alex, put him in charge of Apple Electronics, and gave him a laboratory to come up with new inventions.

Magic Alex showed up in India and found John free of drugs and alcohol, healthier than he had ever been. Despite this, Magic Alex felt something odd was going on, and that the Maharishi was somehow taking advantage of John. It took little detective work to discover that the Maharishi expected the Beatles to give him up to 25 percent of their incomes. His suspicions grew when a pretty American girl confided in Magic Alex that the Maharishi had made inappropriate sexual advances toward her during a private session. After a night of debating, Magic Alex convinced the group to leave the very next day. When the Maharishi asked why, John shot back "You're the cosmic one, you should know."[1] While John was terrified that the Maharishi would put a curse on him, and on the band, he mostly just felt like an idiot for buying into it all. He channeled all his frustrations into a song about the Maharishi, called "Sexy Sadie."

On the flight home, with his new emotions for Yoko, combined with his frustration with the Maharishi, John decided the time was right to tell Cynthia that he had been less than faithful to her—which was an understatement. Cynthia wanted nothing to do with it, saying it was easier to not know. "But you've got to bloody hear it, Cyn," insisted John. Cynthia cried quietly while John regaled her with tales that shattered her innocent naivety, from hundreds of no-name groupies to Joan Baez, playboy bunnies to journalists. "There were an uncountable number," John said heartlessly, "in hotel rooms throughout the world!"[2]

When the plane landed, Cynthia was devastated and hopeless. The only times that John seemed like he might not leave the marriage were when he was high on LSD (which he immediately started

Karma Party: The Beatles go to India to study under the Maharishi, effectively changing the course of their music—and music itself—forever. February 28, 1968. (AP Photo)

taking again upon his return from the ashram). At one point, he even suggested they have more children and fix their lives. Cynthia's emotions swung between hopeful and devastated on a regular basis. Soon, all hope would be lost.

In May, John went to America with Paul to announce the opening of Apple and refused to let Cynthia come with him. Instead, he sent Cynthia away with Jenny Boyd and Magic Alex to Greece, convincing her that a vacation would be good for her, and for their relationship. Cynthia returned from her trip to find John home from America, but not alone. She found John and Yoko in her home, Yoko wearing her bathrobe. The two of them looked up casually, and both said, "Oh. Hi."[3]

***

Yoko Ono means "Ocean Child." She was born in 1933, seven years before John, in Japan. After the war, when Yoko was 12, her family moved to New York where her father had taken a banking job. Yoko was sent to Sarah Lawrence College, where she studied art and music. To the outrage of her family, Yoko was married at 18 to a young Japanese musician, and they moved to Greenwich Village. This was where

Yoko met other artists, poets, and musicians, and fell easily into the New York art scene. She studied Andy Warhol and took up his style of art, which caused outrage, offending audiences that his work be considered art at all.

After a few exhibitions, Yoko moved to London in 1966 with her second husband, an American named Tony Cox, a filmmaker. The two had a daughter, named Kyoko. Yoko gained some fame with her photos of naked rear ends and launched her "Unfinished Paintings and Objects Show," which is where she first met John, having never heard of the Beatles.

John financed her next show, "The Half Wind Show," where all the objects were in half. As the two spent more time together, they got mercilessly caught up in each other. Yoko intrigued John, challenged him, and asserted her opinions openly (a far cry from his polite, agreeable wife); John equally intrigued Yoko, as a man of such power having such insecurity and weakness. John later said:

> I had never known love like this before, and it hit me so hard that I had to halt my marriage to Cynthia . . . With Yoko I really knew love for the first time. When [Yoko] would leave, I'd go back to this sort of suburbia. Then I'd meet her again, and me [*sic*] head would go open like I was on an acid trip.[4]

John had been ready to move from an intellectual friendship to something more since India, when he was writing her letters. With Cynthia in Greece, he decided it was the right time. He invited her over around midnight, and they took LSD together. They listened to John's music in his studio and Yoko praised his artistry. The two decided to make a tape together that night, which consisted mostly of howling, screaming, and breathing. They finished at dawn and then made love for the first time.

It was a few days later that Cynthia returned to find John and Yoko having what appeared to be morning coffee together, at 4 o'clock in the afternoon:

> John and Yoko were sitting on the floor, cross-legged and facing each other, beside a table covered with dirty dishes. . . . John was facing me. He looked at me, expressionless . . . I had no idea how to react. It was clear that he had arranged for me to find them like that and the cruelty of John's betrayal was hard to absorb.

The intimacy between them was daunting. I could feel a wall around them that I could not penetrate.[5]

Cynthia gathered her things and left.

John didn't hesitate: the minute Cynthia walked out the door John began to publicly appear with Yoko. In May 1986, just a few weeks after the confrontation, John brought Yoko to Abbey Road Studios to sit in on their recording. The other Beatles were not overly surprised that John had ended it with Cynthia, and neither were they surprised that John would be cruel enough to appear with another woman almost right away; however, they were shocked and horrified when John brought Yoko into the actual recording room. Not even Brian or George Martin had been allowed to be in the room while the Beatles recorded their music—a silent understanding between them that had existed since the beginning—but suddenly there was Yoko, sitting at John's feet.

Yoko stayed for the whole album, which the Beatles recorded from May to October of 1968. The others attempted to tolerate her, but Yoko managed to push buttons regardless. Not only did she not know the first thing about rock music and therefore never offered anything they considered useful to the conversation, but she literally never went away, not for a moment. The only time they got a moment's peace from her was when John had to go to the washroom, and Yoko would follow him. By the end of recording, the others were completely sick of Yoko, especially Paul. Some might argue that they were "northern boys" and enjoyed their women submissive, quiet, and pretty. Others might sympathize that John had broken a cardinal rule, that when it came to the four of them, everything outside their music was left outside when it came to recording; arguments, grudges, and wives alike. Either way, bringing Yoko inside was like adding a foreign substance to a tried and true formula: it was a very bad reaction, a sort of explosion, one that seemed to break something amongst the band.

John wasn't the only Beatle with romantic turbulence. On Paul and John's trip to America in May, to spread the word about Apple, Paul met up with a rock photographer named Linda Eastman. The two had met briefly on a trip Linda had taken to London in 1967 to photograph the Animals, where they had both ended up at a club called the Bag of Nails, along with other musicians, including Eric Clapton. They struck up a conversation but got separated. Linda managed to get an invitation to the *Sgt. Pepper* photo shoot, where she was found sitting at Paul's feet, snapping his photo over and over again. She was forced to leave with the other photographers and returned to New York infatuated with Paul.

So when Paul went to New York in May of 1968, Linda went to the press conference about Apple and slipped Paul her phone number. Paul called. Linda was a beautiful woman with long blond hair, but hardly any style when compared to, say, Jane Asher. She wore penny loafers and shapeless clothing, and although she would wear short skirts to reveal her attractive long legs, she often appeared unkempt and scruffy. However, her father was a powerful lawyer and Linda was part of the prestigious upper crust of New York—which of course appealed greatly to Paul. In the same way that Jane Asher's family was witty and sophisticated, the Eastmans were wealthy, powerful, and deeply respected.

Paul returned to London, but Jane was on another tour. With Linda in America, and Jane touring, Paul busied himself with a girl who had been hanging around Apple. Paul brought the girl to his home on Cavendish Avenue one night, only to be caught by Jane returning early. A pack of groupies who kept a vigil outside Paul's house day and night attempted to warn him, but he thought they were just joking around. The groupies watched as Jane let herself in and minutes later flew out the door in a fit of rage. Just like Cynthia, Jane had walked in to find another woman in her bathrobe.

Although they were seen together the next day, Jane hardly spoke to Paul again. She went on to be the famous actress she had always wanted to be, eventually got married, and even started a family—everything Paul wanted but didn't want to wait for. However, Paul was not alone for long: Linda Eastman came for a visit, moved in, and never left. With her, she brought her young daughter, Heather, whom Paul adored and treated like his own. Almost instantly it seemed like Paul had the family he'd been wanting for so long.

Cynthia was on vacation in Italy when she saw the photos in the paper of John and Yoko together, and she took to bed for days. The son of the owners of the hotel, Roberto, was procured to take Cynthia out, and the two went out on the town. After a night jumping from club to club, and after far too many drinks, they returned in the early hours of the morning to find a man waiting for Cynthia: Magic Alex. John had sent Alex to inform Cynthia that he was filing for divorce on the grounds of adultery, of all things. Alex had agreed to testify if it went to trial, and informed Cynthia that he would claim the two of them had been intimate, and also pointed out that her stumbling home with Roberto wouldn't look good either.

When Cynthia returned to London, she had to wait two full weeks to get a meeting with John, and even then, Yoko was present. Cynthia, humiliated to discuss the matters in front of Yoko. John didn't want to hear it and told her that in order for him to avoid bad publicity, she should let him claim adultery, after which he would give her a small sum of money for a settlement. Cynthia let him.

The charges were dropped when John and Yoko found out Yoko was pregnant in September. Cynthia was then able to sue John on the same grounds, and the case was settled for a mere £100,000. Cynthia bought a home and moved on with her life. One of the few people that ever came to see her from her old life was Paul, who felt so bad for her that he even offered to marry her. To cheer up little Julian, who missed the dad he hardly knew, Paul wrote him a little song: "Hey Julian, it's not so bad / take a sad song, and make it better." This song would, of course, go on to be "Hey Jude."

Yoko didn't think she was able to get pregnant, as she had had several abortions and was nine years older than John. She and John had spent the summer in Ringo's old flat, using it as a lover's hide-away, where Yoko introduced John to the wonders of heroin. They spent the summer lying on the floor, high and useless, but, apparently, becoming pregnant. John's new love for heroin was blamed solely on Yoko by everyone in John's life, viewed as just another way Yoko could control him.

Cynthia was gone. John was on heroin. Yoko was pregnant. Paul had left Jane. Fans were upset. What else could go wrong? The answer was Apple Corps. While on their trip to America back in May, where John and Paul had announced the opening of Apple, they had also made a call to artists everywhere:

> We really want to help people, but without doing it like a charity or seeming like ordinary patrons of the arts. I mean, we're in the happy position of not really needing any more money, so for the first time, the bosses aren't for profit. If you come to see me and said "I've had such and such a dream," I will say, "Here's so much money. Go away and do it."[6]

Little did they know the storm they would create with those very words.

In the meantime, almost as a symbol of what was to come, the Apple Boutique was closed. It turned out that the only thing the store was good for was shoplifting, and each day more clothes went missing as hippies came and went as they pleased. The Fool had pretty well disappeared after angry letters from the accountants showed they had lost £200,000 in just seven months. The clothing was liquidated—mostly to Yoko, but also in a free-for-all—and the doors were closed.

But instead of giving up, the Beatles moved on to what they assumed would be bigger and better things. They purchased a much bigger office space: a five-story Georgian-styled townhouse. Located at 3 Savile Row, it had cost £500,000, and they had it decorated with apple green carpet, fireplaces, funky chandeliers, and expensive wood furniture. It was a full house: the first floor was reception, and Ron Kass's office; The second floor was offices for the Beatles, Neil, and Peter Brown; the third floor was for press and publicity, with Derek Taylor's office, as well as a kitchen with two chefs; the fourth floor was for all the various veins of Apple, such as film, talent, music, accounting, and so on; the basement was for Magic Alex and his electronics department, where he was working on a state-of-the-art recording studio.

Everything seemed to be looking up; it was all so shiny and new. However, the call that John and Paul had made in America had spread to papers and magazines everywhere. They even had a poster made of a street performer (it was actually Alistair Taylor) with all sorts of instruments, titled "This Man Had Talent," and went on to say how he had sent his tape to Apple and now owned a Bentley. The Beatles had the poster sent to all the papers and posted everywhere, and soon enough, "artists" started showing up: hippies who wanted to start colonies and communes; acid-heads who wanted to research new drugs; crazies who claimed to be prophets or messiahs; and every kind of artist under the sun. Tapes, films, paintings, letters, and photos began pouring in, and Apple Corps began cutting checks.

The summer of 1968 was the height of all this madness, with Apple Corps full of wandering bohemian idealists, while the Beatles were still busy in the recording studio pumping out song after song. In August they released "Hey Jude" / "Revolution," and the combination would go on to be their best-selling single. "Hey Jude" had stemmed from a little ditty Paul had originally come up with to comfort Julian, after John had left. The B-side, "Revolution," was a second-take on one of John's songs. The message—which was a stance against the war in Vietnam, but also against violent antiwar protestors—was confusing, with John saying both "count me out" and "count me in." Regardless, the song went on to be a huge success among activists and protesters.

Everything seemed to be looking up, with "Hey Jude" on its way to selling six million copies, when on October 18, the police showed up at Ringo's old flat, to bust John and Yoko. Seven cops showed up with a search warrant and a dog and managed to scrounge up about an ounce and a half of pot. John and Yoko were arrested. They were released on bail thanks to Sir Joseph Lockwood, the chairman of EMI, who pleaded on their behalf.

John and Yoko harnessed all the attention the drug bust stirred up and focused it on the release of an album they had made. It was the music the two of them had recorded the first time Yoko had come over, when they tripped on acid all night long. The music would be considered experimental at best, and a headache at worst. They titled it *Unfinished Music No. 1—Two Virgins,* since after recording it they had consummated their relationship for the first time.

However, it wasn't the music that was about to make such a fuss, so much as the cover. It was "art," John and Yoko argued, but the executives at EMI wanted nothing to do with it. Standing in front of a bed, with their arms wrapped around each other, were John and Yoko, completely naked. EMI begged John and Yoko to reconsider, but they wouldn't budge. The album was grudgingly released on November 11 (just three days after John and Cynthia's divorce was finalized) and had to be displayed and sold in a paper bag. John and Yoko might have put up a fuss about this, except that Yoko had a miscarriage that month. John stayed by Yoko's bed in the hospital through the night, sleeping on the floor. They were completely devastated.

On November 13, the Beatles' third movie was released: *Yellow Submarine.* The band had signed a contract back in the days of *A Hard Day's Night* that required three films to be completed (the second film was *Help!*). However, by the time the third film was due, they had no interest in wasting their time that way. So instead a cartoon was made, featuring the animated Beatles on a wacky adventure, and dubbed over by voice actors imitating the Beatles. With nearly nothing to go with the cartoon, the film did well and appeased fans who had been so disappointed by *Magical Mystery Tour* (which was independent and didn't count in the three-film contract).

But more important than John and Yoko's solo project, or a Beatle cartoon, was the release of their next album, destined to be historic. It had taken nearly six months to record, a turbulent year of divorces, pregnancies, drug busts, Apple Corps, and, of course, John and Yoko. The album was officially called *The Beatles,* but it was hard to tell, as the record was encased in a simple, shiny, white cover with a small stamp that read "The Beatles." It was their only double album.

Informally dubbed the *White Album*, it was received with huge success in both the United Kingdom and America, and it went straight to number one. It was hailed as a musical success, although it certainly had its flaws. Between Paul's overbearing direction and John's angry tantrums, the two stopped writing songs together. In the past, they had each relied on the other to polish off a song in that classic Lennon-McCartney style; now they were each producing songs all on their own, often without that special "something" the other used to add. As well, there was a tension, created by both Paul's dictatorship and Yoko's presence, that managed to come across in the music. And, of course, John's worsening heroin condition only made everything harder.

This tension created an album that was a collaboration of four individuals, rather than the unity of a band, as had been seen on *Revolver* and *Sgt Pepper*. Stereotypically, John's songs were full of angst, discontentment, and rebellion, while Paul's songs were introspective, poetic, and "happier." Still, both of them were experimenting in their own ways. John wrote "Julia" in the same style that Paul had written "Yesterday," with a soft melody and nostalgic overtone, which also appeared in "Dear Prudence," apparently written about Mia Farrow's sister back in India. Paul lashed out with "Helter Skelter" (a song later said to have "inspired" Charles Manson) and "Why Don't We Do It In The Road."

There was "Back In The U.S.S.R.," which was a parody inspired by both Chuck Berry and the Beach Boys' "California Girls." John also wrote a parody, except his was aimed at extreme Beatle fans, called "Glass Onion." The song was written in response to the ridiculous hidden messages fans had "found" in Beatle lyrics, or by playing records backward, and referenced "Strawberry Fields Forever," "I Am the Walrus," "Lady Madonna," "Fool on the Hill," and "Fixing a Hole," most notably singing "The walrus was Paul."

Paul unleashed a heart-wrenching song, as beautiful as it was dark, which managed to universally affect listeners. Paul said he had written the song in response to the civil rights movement, about a black woman, "bird" being a term for a girl; hence, "Blackbird." Eerie but hopeful, the song resounded with the times, and with the people, in a very lasting way.

George had written a song that was arguably as good as a John or Paul tune, called "While My Guitar Gently Weeps." A lamenting, sad song with a heavy guitar behind it, it included riffs by George's pal Eric Clapton, of Cream. The song was a triumph, and George received much praise for it, both lyrically and musically.

With the *White Album* having 30 songs, it was a musical mish-mash of four souls trying to break free from one another: John was angry and lashing out, Paul was confident and controlling, George was frustrated and smothered, and Ringo was insecure and feeling unneeded. Still, when the four souls collided, they created an explosion that bore new life and new creations. The *White Album* was a great success for a band on its way to falling apart.

***

It was Paul's idea, really. Paul was a born performer: he lived for the thrill of the crowd, the attention, the adventure and spontaneity of live music. After nearly three years, Paul was aching to perform again and began talking of different tours they could do. With the other three Beatles completely against it, Paul desperately suggested just one big show, to keep a connection with the fans. One big show sounded okay to the group, but just one. Then they could record it and release it as a live album: a live concert to send to their fans around the world.

Ideas flew around this idea of one show: everything from a small pub, to the African desert, to New York, to a television station, to an ocean liner, to Hollywood bowl was suggested. While they waited for the perfect idea to present itself, the four of them decided to get to work on rehearsing for what would be their first show in three years. They decided to film their time rehearsing too, perhaps to use during the to-be-determined concert, or to release later as a documentary along with the album.

On January 2, 1969, the four of them entered Twickenham Studios, met by a film crew headed up by Michael Lindsay-Hogg, a director. The film was originally to be called *Get Back,* as a reference to getting back to their roots. The opening scene revealed a friendly atmosphere among the Beatles, as they puffed out their chests and barreled through songs like they were teenagers again, even bringing back a Quarrymen tune, "The One after 909." Together they jammed through their old list of songs by favorite musicians, such as Chuck Berry, Little Richard, and Elvis. They laughed together and goofed off around the large, empty rehearsal room. There was a glimmer of hope for reigniting the passion they had all once shared.

Early on in the film, the camera reveals Yoko standing almost right behind John, watching him intently. Just like with the *White Album,* Yoko was always next to John, eerily close and almost never taking her gaze from him. It is easy to imagine why bringing her into the recording room was frustrating and irritating for the other Beatles. As irritating as having Yoko around again must have been, even worse was Paul's overbearing dictatorship over the music. He was constantly correcting the others, especially George, which escalated the tension more than Yoko ever could. By January 10, just eight days after entering Twickenham Studios, George snapped: he stood up, grabbed his guitar, threw on his jacket, and walked out the door.

When George left, Paul and John acted as if it was no big deal, even cattily suggesting that they call Eric Clapton. Of course, John was bluffing—the Beatles was the four of them and no one else. No one could actually replace a Beatle. So a series of meetings was held to discuss what could be done to make George return. George's demands were simple, but harsh: leave Twickenham Studios, and give up on the live concert idea. Leaving Twickenham was not an issue—the studio was large, had too many echoes, and was freezing cold—and organizing a big show was becoming too much of a hassle anyway. They agreed to continue recording in the Apple Studio that Magic Alex had built (actually, the studio he built was a complete disaster and George Martin had to be called in to fix it).

It was January 22 when the recording restarted. They ran through all their old favorites, bursting out into long jams when they felt like it. John and Paul reconnected for a few sweet moments during the recording of "The Two of Us," a song written about the early days of Paul and Linda's relationship. Watching the film, one cannot help but feel a connection between Paul and John as they stand side by side, sharing a microphone and exchanging smiles and chuckles while belting out the catchy love song in perfect harmony: "You and I have memories / longer than the road that stretches out ahead."

On January 29, after being back for a week, the film crew was discussing how to wrap up the film if there was to be no concert. With no ideas, the conversation turned to how lovely the Apple offices were, and Ringo mentioned the pretty rooftop garden. A light bulb went off for John: a rooftop concert. It had never been done, and it was easy. Lindsay-Hogg loved the idea, and the rest of the Beatles were easily won over as well. Preparations were made to play the very next day.

January 30, 1969, would be the very last live performance by the Beatles, ever, and it would last all of 42 minutes. Although the Beatles couldn't quite be seen, speakers boomed through the streets, and they could certainly be heard. They stood there brimming with more excitement than any of them had had in a while, and they launched into "Get Back," which they played four times throughout the 42 minutes. "Get Back" was originally a reference to getting back to their roots, but had become a satire on politics and racism toward immigrants ("Get Back to where you once belonged"). They also played three versions of "Don't Let Me Down," which John claimed was a love song about Yoko ("I'm in love for the first time") but the band thought was about his addiction to heroin, and that "Don't let me down!" was a cry for help. There were two versions of "I've Got a Feeling," and just one take of "The One after 909," and "Dig a Pony," as well as an instrumental version of "God Save the Queen."

The music was loud. Within the first song, people working on the street (mostly tailors and businessmen) were gathering to figure out what was happening. Soon, phone calls were made and word spread like wildfire that the Beatles were playing a free show from their roof—their first show in three years. They were back! Screaming girls came from all directions; people working nearby climbed onto their roofs; traffic came to a complete standstill. Most of the hundreds of people gathering on the streets were bewildered and fascinated, in a kind of state of shock. Of course, not everyone was pleased, and soon the phones were ringing off the hooks at the local police station. Police arrived to direct traffic, keep people back, and tell the Beatles to shut it down.

Surprisingly, *Get Back* was shelved at the time due to the overwhelming amount of video footage and recordings, and the disappointing sound quality (both at Twickenham and Apple Studios, and on the roof). Since the Beatles were determined to put "live" songs on the album, they had to get a song all in one take—which usually took them 50 or 60 tries to get right. This left 29 hours of footage of different takes. The film and album were renamed *Let It Be,* which was exactly what happened: both the footage and the album were left alone for the time being, as nobody was ready to tackle the mess. The task was too daunting for the moment, and *Let It Be* was left behind.

NOTES

1. Quoted in Peter Brown and Steven Gaines, *The Love You Make: An Insider's Story of the Beatles* (New York: McGraw-Hill Book Company, 1976), 289.
2. Ibid., 291.
3. Quoted in Cynthia Lennon, *John* (New York: Random House, 2005), 295.
4. Quoted in Keith Badman, *The Beatles: Off The Record* (New York: Music Sales Corp., 2000), 363.
5. Quoted in Lennon, *John*, 295.
6. Quoted on *The Tonight Show Starring Johnny Carson,* TV Series, Frederick De Cordova (New York City, NBC, May 15, 1968).

CHAPTER TEN

Let It Be

I'm leaving the group.

John Lennon

Allen Klein had had his eye on Beatles since 1964. He was an American accountant from New York, who was famous for renegotiating musicians' percentages and advances. In 1965 he became the comanager of the Rolling Stones, and in 1966 he bought them out from Andrew Loog Oldham. Allen earned a reputation as a cut-throat businessman, but also as a man not to be trusted, with a variety of lawsuits in his wake. When Brian died in 1967, Allen waited quietly for the right moment to move in on the Beatles. He knew Brian had been the voice of conscience with the band when it came to spending; without him, the Beatles were bound to waste their money and need a hand up. Allen was ready to be just that hand.

He only had to wait until 1969, when John was quoted saying, "We did it all wrong—Paul and me running to New York saying, 'We'll do this and encourage this and that.' . . . if it carries on like this, all of us will be broke in six months."[1] He was referring to the sad state of Apple, where money was being handed out like candy, to hippies and employees alike. The Beatles had had money problems before Brian had died, but it was nothing compared to the amount moving through Apple, "Eighteen or twenty thousand pounds a week was rolling out . . . and nobody was doing anything about it."[2]

Allen pounced. He called Apple repeatedly, but the band was busy at Twickenham, recording *Get Back*. Relentless, Allen finally got through to John—whom he targeted as not only the leader, but the most disgruntled—and arranged a meeting. John and Yoko went together and met Allen at the Dorchester Hotel on January 28, 1969 to discuss the Beatles' impending financial doom. Allen played John from every angle: he displayed vast knowledge of Beatles music, especially John's lyrics; he had done his research and had a very firm grasp of the problems facing the band; and, perhaps most important, he asked Yoko for her opinion. This last tactic was key, for nothing infuriated John more than the other Beatles' obvious disdain for Yoko, how they ignored her and wanted her to remain as much in the background as possible. Allen also hit home with John by showing up not in a suit, but in a sweater and sneakers; by portraying his New York street sense that was akin to Liverpool's; and by sharing that he too had lost his mother as a child and had grown up with an aunt. John practically crawled into Allen's lap for a hug. That very day he wrote to Sir Joseph Lockwood, EMI's chairman, "Dear Sir Joe—from now on, Allen Klein handles all my stuff."[3]

This, of course, came as a shock to the band for two reasons: first, no member of the Beatles had struck out on his own to make such a huge decision, and the others felt baffled and betrayed by John's actions; second, everyone assumed the band already had someone to deal with their financial situation. Linda's father, Lee Eastman, was a prominent and revered New York show business attorney, who specialized in international copyrights pertaining to the entertainment industry, and he seemed not only appropriate for the job, but the most likely candidate considering Paul and Linda were together. Eastman was a shoo-in.

Lee sent his son, John Eastman, to take care of the meetings. The topic up for discussion was what to do about Nemporer Holdings, which was the new NEMS being run by Clive Epstein, and which was still taking album royalties, along with Brian's 25 percent. They all knew Clive was torn, because he wished to retain control over the company for his brother's sake, but he could not pay out Brian's massive debt that he had left behind. Essentially, Clive was finally ready to hear offers for his share in the company. He had been approached by Triumph Investment Trust, and an offer was presented of one million pounds. John Eastman's idea was to match Triumph's offer. Sir

Joseph at EMI had agreed to advance the money to the Beatles, and Clive felt like the Beatles were entitled to the share. The plan was to buy out the Epstein family, as well as Dick James, who owned the other major share of NEMS, as well as John and Paul's song-writing company that they had formed in 1963, Northern Songs. To pull this off, it was agreed that John Eastman and Allen Klein would work together on the project, although Allen was secretly plotting how to commandeer the whole thing.

Allen began with an audit of their state of financial affairs. He found that EMI had the Beatles locked into a nine-year contract and NEMS was taking profits and Brian's cut, Dick James was making huge money from Northern Songs, and Apple was failing miserably. Meanwhile, Lee Eastman returned to London to meet with the Beatles and Allen. In the meeting, Allen used his foul mouth and bluntness to attack Lee until he snapped. Lee stood up shouting right back at Allen and threw a total fit, which was, of course, exactly what Allen was hoping for. Lee Eastman had walked right into his trap. Allen had successfully made Lee Eastman look unstable, immature, and weak. It was now only Paul who sided with Lee Eastman, and the other three were with Allen Klein.

Both Lee and Allen moved into the Apple house to continue working on winning NEMS. The first thing Allen did was make cuts. People were fired left, right, and center at Apple, both newer, lazy employees, and old, die-hard irreplaceable ones, such as Alistair Taylor. Also on the chopping block were the excess divisions: Apple Films, Apple Publishing, Apple Retail, and Magic Alex's disastrous Apple Electronics were all shut down.

Once these changes had taken place, Allen began work on the deal with NEMS and Nemporer Holdings. Unfortunately, John Eastman had already gotten there, on behalf of Paul's interests, and had made a superb mess of things. Eastman had written a letter to Clive Epstein, asking him to meet to discuss "Mr. Klein's audit as well as the propriety of the negotiations . . . between EMI, and the Beatles, and NEMS."[4] Clive had been deeply offended by the word "propriety," which suggested his company's—and his brother's—ethics were being questioned. Instead of responding to Eastman, Clive decided to sell his 70 percent of Nemporer to Triumph Holdings, quickly. In doing this, Triumph received the right to pocket Brian's 25 percent of royalties and received a stake in Northern Songs as well.

The Beatles had lost not only a large chunk of their income to a soulless corporation, but they had also lost a chance at creative and financial control of their work. It infuriated them that a corporation—men in suits!—would be taking what would be a massive sum of their money over the next seven years, until the agreement could be renegotiated. Klein attempted to bully Triumph into selling, making threats that NEMS back-owed the Beatles for more than the company was worth. When Allen was thrown out of Triumph's office, he wrote to Sir Joseph at EMI stating that royalties needed to be paid directly to Apple Corps.

Sir Joseph had already begun the process of paying out more than £1 million back-owed to the Beatles and found himself torn between honoring the Beatles, who had made him vast sums of money, and honoring the legal contract with Triumph. Instead of making such a hard decision, Sir Joseph sent the matter to the courts and put a hold on the money. The courts, however, did little to solve the problem. In the end, Allen was able to get Triumph to sell NEMS for 800 thousand pounds plus one quarter of the pending royalties. The financial blow was large, but the royalties in the long run would be massive, so it was a good deal for the Beatles.

Although they had obtained control over Nemporer and gained financial freedom, there were still more roadblocks ahead. Northern Songs was one of the most popular stocks in London, making the band, and their shareholders, lots of money. Dick James, their old producer, who had originally encouraged John and Paul to form their company in 1963, decided to sell his large share in Northern Songs to a company called ATV. He did it without so much as offering a chance to buy to the band that had made him a fortune.

Dick later claimed he had done it for the good of the band. Yes, Dick was indebted to the Fab Four for bringing in millions in revenue, but he was also responsible to the several thousand shareholders who had staked money in Northern Songs, which was a very popular stock. Lately those shareholders had become uncomfortable with the events transpiring around the most troubled Beatle, John. His estrangement and divorce from Cynthia; his public relationship with Yoko that involved nude album covers and drug charges; his fling with the Maharishi; his known addiction to heroin; and his wild "happenings" that he and Yoko staged were all events that caused shareholders much unease. Finally, there was Allen Klein's dubious reputation, with lawsuits still pending, including one from the Rolling Stones.

All this anxiety was too much for poor Dick to bear, and when Allen Klein came into the picture, Dick caved. He sold to Lew Grade, his old theatrical agent, who owned ATV and was already a minority shareholder in Northern Songs. Dick sold his 23 percent for over one million pounds, giving ATV 35 percent altogether; ATV immediately bid a massive £9 million for the rest of the company.

The deal could not have gone through at a worse time: both Paul and John had just gotten married and gone on their honeymoons. Paul went first, marrying Linda Eastman on March 11. Paul leaked the news the day before, and hoards of weepy girls made the pilgrimage to witness the desolate occasion, their sobs ringing through the streets for days. While fans were still recovering, John and Yoko decided to make the leap only eight days later. They were on vacation in France when they decided to get married and flew to the island of Gibraltar (a British colony) to avoid any visa conflicts, and Peter Brown flew out to be the best man. They were married and flew back to Paris the same day.

Instead of a lovely honeymoon in Paris, John and Yoko staged a "happening" in Amsterdam. *Happening* was a recently popular term for almost any kind of unprogrammed, "organic" event, and, in this case, the happening was a "bed-in" at the Amsterdam Hilton. While they lay in bed in their pajamas, reporters came and went, and John and Yoko spoke about being propeace and antiwar, and, much to the disappointment of the press, it was all quite tame (however, many were baffled by how lying down in a luxurious bed had anything to do with stopping war).

On March 28, day three of the bed-in, John opened the newspaper to discover the horrifying fact that Dick James had sold his share in Northern Songs. The betrayal was thick. As John read the news in the daily paper from his bed-in in Amsterdam, the fury of it all nearly ruined his entire "antiviolence" protest. From his bed, John addressed the press: "I won't sell!" he snapped, "These are my shares and my songs. . . . I know damn well [Paul] feels the same as I do."[5]

Allen began his next big undertaking, returning Northern Songs back to its rightful owners. The Beatles, collectively, owned 31.6 percent of the company (John and Paul had 15 percent each, while Ringo and George shared 1.6 percent), and Allen's plan was to scrounge up enough money to buy out another 20 percent, putting them back as the majority shareholder. He scrambled to find £2 million from various Beatle companies and investments and began the long, drawn-out meetings with ATV. By May of 1969, Lew Grade and ATV were ready to make a deal, exhausted from the battle with Allen; however, John showed up one day and stated that he was tired of being "fucked

Give Peace a Chance: John Lennon and his new wife Yoko Ono spend their honeymoon staging a "bed-in" in Amsterdam, promoting peace and condemning war. March 25, 1969. (AP Photo)

around by men in suits."[6] Offended, ATV decided not to sell, and the whole case collapsed. ATV not only kept its 35 percent of Northern Songs but acquired the extra 20 percent needed to put them at the majority, with 55 percent. Northern Songs was no longer theirs—although admittedly, it hadn't been for a long time.

***

May 9, 1969, was a busy day. First of all, it was the opening and christening of Zapple, the experimental music arm of their record company. Along with the opening came the release of two albums: *Electronic Sound* by George, a mainly instrumental album, and *Unfinished Music No 2—Life with the Lions*, by John and Yoko, an experimental album. *Life with the Lions* featured a private photo, much like their last album had, of the Ono Lennons (in a private ceremony the month before, John had taken Ono as his middle name, and Yoko had added Lennon to hers). Instead of nakedness, the photo showed the couple in the hospital—Yoko in the bed, and John on the floor—during Yoko's miscarriage in November of 1968. One song on the album was "Baby's Heartbeat," which was a recording of the actual failing heartbeat of the baby the pair had lost. On the album's listings, the heartbeat is credited to "John Ono Lennon II."

Their album didn't even touch U.K. charts and barely showed up on the U.S. ones. Despite the flop, the couple, mildly offended, carried on with their other "happenings," such as appearing in bags ("bagism" they called it, which allowed for "total communication" regardless of appearance, sex, race, etc.) and releasing a film called *Rape,* which looked at the media's intrusion into people's lives. Their next "big" happening, however, was another bed-in. This time the bed-in was in Canada, as they were denied entrance to the United States—their first choice—on the grounds of drug charges. They rerouted to the Queen Elizabeth Hotel in Montreal and climbed into bed on May 26, opening their doors to the press. While there they summoned a troupe of friends, among them Timothy and Rosemary Leary, Murray the K, Derek Taylor, and Allen Ginsberg, and set up a makeshift studio to record a song they had written, called "Give Peace a Chance." It would be John's first independent single that would have success, although he would regret giving the writing credits to Lennon-McCartney, and not to Yoko. It went on to be released July 4, 1969.

Before "Give Peace a Chance" came out, the Beatles released two singles. They decided to salvage something from the wreck that was *Let It Be* and pulled two songs to be edited and released. "Get Back"/ "Don't Let Me Down" hit the charts on April 11, and, of course, it went straight to number one. The second, and more surprising single, was when the band agreed to release John's "The Ballad of John and Yoko," which was John's response to Paul's "Two of Us," chronicling John and Yoko's marriage and honeymoon. It was recorded almost single-handedly by John, except for Paul on drums. Use of the word "Christ" in the chorus ("Christ, you know it ain't easy!") caused the song to be banned immediately from radio play, but the single went on to have good commercial success, and it made John happy to have a song that included Yoko in the Beatle's repertoire. It was released in the United Kingdom, with George's song "Old Brown Shoe" on the B-side, on May 30.

Once they had put out some singles, the next thing to tackle was whether or not there was going to be another album. The footage from *Let It* Be was now set to be a movie and would not be ready for another year; therefore, an album also couldn't be released for a year. Even though John and Paul could hardly stand each other, it was agreed that they should give recording one more try. For the most part, they just needed the money, but Paul had also suggested that they make an album the way they used to, back in the days of *Rubber Soul*, which was an attractive idea to the other Beatles. John had been dying to make music for months, but all the legal hassles had made it nearly impossible, so he was more than ready to hit the studio, even if it was with Paul. They called in George Martin, and he agreed to the project, so long as he was allowed to produce it the way he used to. No more attempts to record a song "live" and in one take (as they often took 50 takes, or more, to get it perfect); instead, overdubbing, editing, and mixing had to come back into play. The bulk of the recording was done throughout the summer of 1969.

The recording had a rocky start: on July 1, John and Yoko, along with Kyoko and Julian, had been in a terrible car accident while driving to Scotland on a family trip. The sole cause of this was the fact that John had been driving—John, who hadn't driven since he was a teenager and had been chauffeured for the last six years. John required 17 stitches, Yoko needed 14, Kyoko needed four, and Julian was unscathed but needed treatment for shock. The car was demolished, but John had it shipped to his and Yoko's new home, Tittenhurst Park, where it was mounted like a piece of art.

So when John and Yoko entered Abbey Road Studios to join the Beatles, they were slightly shaken up. Yoko required a bed to lie in, which had a microphone suspended from the ceiling so that she could continue to comment on the music—this once again caused tension among the rest of the band, although they were getting used to the constant annoyance. Despite this, the recording actually went along quite well. Perhaps it was John's brush with death that inspired him to carry on amicably with the Beatles; perhaps it was the comfort of returning to the place where they had recorded so much of their best work; or perhaps it was the simple knowledge that this was, almost definitely, the last time the Beatles would ever work together.

The album would prove to be possibly the best work of their careers. This is mostly because they had simply grown as musicians, had peaked artistically, on personal levels. One might argue that *Rubber Soul* and *Revolver* were their tightest works as a group, whereas this album was arguably their best work as four individual musicians. The most obvious example was the rise of George Harrison to a level no one expected him to reach: "Here Comes the Sun" was possibly the most popular song on the whole album, and "Something" was on a par with any song by the Lennon-McCartney duo. Lyrically, "Something" was universally applicable and almost perfectly described the mystery of true love: "Something in the way she moves / attracts me like no other lover." It was easily on the same level as "Yesterday" or "Here, There, and Everywhere." George had caught fire as his own musician and had finally stepped out of the shadows of John and Paul.

John came around with a song inspired by a slogan he had originally written for Timothy Leary's campaign for governor of California: "Come Together." Leary had abandoned his campaign, so John kept the slogan and turned it into a cheeky song full of inside jokes and private references. The chorus was overtly sexual with "Come together / right now, over me," but more disturbing for avid listeners was John's hook after the chorus. On the recording, it sounds like "Shooook," but in reality what John was really singing was an eerie foreshadowing: "Shoot Me!"

Another song formulated by John was actually very impromptu. Yoko was playing Beethoven's "Moonlight Sonata" on piano when John asked her to play it backward. What developed was the music for "Because," a song of pure harmony. George, Paul, and John sang the three-part harmony, which was overdubbed twice, creating a nine-part symphony of voices. Such beautiful harmony would hardly allude to the tension and resentment brewing underneath.

Paul was overthrown as the leader, and his usually large contribution was reduced to three songs; surprisingly, two of them were not very good at all. The issue of Paul's strange deterioration in songwriting went unspoken at the time, but later in his career, it would resurface and follow him long after the Beatles were done. The one good song was "You Never Give Me Your Money," directed explicitly at Allen Klein. Then there was "Oh! Darling" and "Maxwell's Silver Hammer." "Oh! Darling" was, essentially, very boring; "Maxwell's Silver Hammer" was a pop-song with dark, odd lyrics about a fellow named Maxwell bludgeoning his wife to death with a hammer.

The album also consisted of a medley of six unfinished songs: "Sun King" and "Mean Mr. Mustard," both of which were stabs at '60s culture; "Polythene Pam" and "She Came in through the Bathroom Window," the first being about an affair John had where the woman involved enjoyed being wrapped in plastic bags, and the second being about a crazed fan; and "Golden Slumbers" and "Carry that Weight," the first being inspired by a 400-year-old Thomas Dekker poem, and the second being about the awful weight of being a Beatle. On the original album, these songs are listed as six separate titles, but each pair was recorded in one session.

Since the idea behind the album was do it like they used to, they decided to name the album after the place to which they owed so much of their success: *Abbey Road*. For a cover, they simply walked outside and crossed the street. It was a simple moment at the time: John happened to be wearing white, a sort of trend he and Yoko had going; Paul, at the last minute, decided to kick off his shoes. Yet these seemingly simple actions, as with many Beatles actions, would go on to be immortalized, and to be copied for decades to come. The end of recording the album was marked by the birth of Paul's first child, a little girl named Mary, on August 28.

During the recording of *Abbey Road*, John had begun his exit. He had been planning to leave the band for a while but was convinced by Allen Klein to stay, so that the band continued to make money. So instead of leaving, he and Yoko moved in. When Allen fired Ron Kass at Apple, John and Yoko took Ron's office on the first floor. They formed their own company, called Bag Productions, through which they sponsored and endorsed their own "happenings." Aside from the bagism and bed-ins, and avant-garde films about John's penis (called *Self-Portrait*), they also built robots. These robots were made up of the best recording equipment available at the time, and they were christened "The Plastic Ono Band." The idea was that John and Yoko would form a band that, unlike the Beatles, was not pinned down to specific musicians; instead, it would fluctuate with whoever was around to make music, musicians or not, and be recorded on the robots. The first song attributed to the Plastic Ono Band was "Give Peace a Chance," although the robots were not present for the recording.

The second song for the Plastic Ono Band was "Cold Turkey." Throughout 1968, John and Yoko had been doing heroin on a regular basis. By 1969, John, especially, appeared to be on death's doorstep, with his pale skin, sunken eyes, and long, greasy hair. Late in the summer, during the final recording of *Abbey Road*, John and Yoko decided to start trying to get pregnant again; therefore, they had to quit heroin. They did it at home, in private, which is where John wrote "Cold Turkey." Then in September John received an invitation to the Toronto Rock 'n' Roll Revival Festival. He gathered together Klaus Voorman (his old friend from Hamburg who played bass), Eric Clapton, and Alan White, a drummer, and they left the very next day for a 24-hour stint in Canada.

It was on the plane that John realized he had not played to live audience in three years. He was nervous, edgy, and even threw up before going on stage, but it proved to be worthwhile. John had a blast playing with Eric and the others, being on stage, and performing for an audience. Yoko sat on the stage in a bag, singing along. They flew home the next day. At some point during the 24-hour adventure, John had realized something: it wasn't live performances he hated; it was performing with the Beatles that he hated. And so, on the flight home, to a group of tired friends, John announced that he was leaving the Beatles.

Shortly after John returned home, *Abbey Road* was released; also, Allen had renegotiated their deal with Capitol Records to a massive (at the time) 69 cents per album. The deal went through on September 20, and *Abbey Road* was released September 26. The band had to get together to sign the new deal, which was where John hastily informed the rest of the Beatles that he was leaving. Paul had been rambling on about doing some gigs again, but John had had enough of pretending that he was sticking around: "Klein asked me not to tell you but . . . I'm leaving the group."[7] Everyone was stunned. Since both George and John had claimed they were leaving, everyone hoped John was bluffing, but at the same time, everyone knew he wasn't. Paul and Allen convinced John, once again, not to say anything, so that it didn't interfere with the sales of *Abbey Road*.

In order to distract himself from the messiness of the break-up, John threw himself into his activism, into the Plastic Ono Band, and into Bag Productions. On October 24, the Plastic Ono Band released "Cold Turkey" as its second single. It was the first song officially credited to John alone, and to the Plastic Ono Band, with no links to Lennon-McCartney. The B-side of the album was a song by Yoko called "Don't Worry Kyoko (Mummy's Only Looking for a Hand in the Snow." The single would peak at only #14 on the U.K. charts, and #30 in the United States. In November, amidst many other "happenings," John protested against the royal family by returning his MBE, along with a note:

Your Majesty,

I am returning my MBE as a protest against Britain's involvement in the Nigeria-Biafra thing, against our support of America in Vietnam and against "Cold Turkey" slipping down the charts.

With Love,

John Lennon[8]

Despite the letter, "Cold Turkey" continued to slip in the charts and eventually disappeared. Ironically, one of the songs that pushed it out of the way was a new single by The Beatles. "Something" / "Come Together" was released one week after "Cold Turkey," on October 31, and rocketed straight to number one.

John and Yoko then released their third album, *Wedding Album.* The A-side consisted of John and Yoko shouting each other's names; the B-side was clips from interviews at the Montreal bed-in. The album didn't even make the charts in the United Kingdom and peaked at number 178 in the United States. After their third flop in a row, one might think they would have given up. Instead, they pulled together the recorded tapes from Toronto and released *Live Peace in Toronto 1969* on December 12—after much persuading at EMI— and surprisingly, the album went to number 10 in the United States.

The year came to an end with the premiere of a movie starring Ringo, called *The Magic Christian*, with John being selected as Man of the Year by *Rolling Stone Magazine,* and with John and Yoko revealing their "War Is Over" campaign. Huge billboard-sized signs were dropped in numerous cities around the world that read "War is Over, if you want it. Happy Christmas, love John and Yoko." Then they capped off a decade by giving themselves a buzz cut, sacrificing their precious hair for the sake of what they called "Year One for Peace." Sadly, war was not over, but as John's famous and symbolic hair hit the floor, two things certainly were: the 1960s, and the Beatles.

It was a swift descent. The year 1970 began with a display of John's lithographs, which were scenes from their honeymoon as well as "private" semierotic drawings of Yoko, being confiscated from the London Arts Gallery on grounds of being obscene. In February of 1970, the Plastic Ono Band continued to ride its popularity with a new single called "Instant Karma," with a B-side by Yoko called "Who Has Seen the Wind?" The flexible band still featured Klaus Voorman and Alan White, but with an addition of Mal Evans, Billy Preston, and George Harrison. "Instant Karma" was a success in sales and even received radio play.

All four Beatles were sitting quietly on the fact that the band was broken up, waiting for *Let It Be* to be released. The wealth of material sitting in Apple had been adopted by an infamous producer who was willing to take on the enormous task of editing it: Phil Spector, who had been on the plane with them the day they first flew to America in 1964. Phil arrived to save the day and spent months putting together the album—as well as working with the Plastic Ono Band—while

Lindsay-Hogg worked on the film. Phil brought in his technique of creating a "wall of sound" and dubbed, redubbed, and overlaid various recordings until he had something that sounded like a song. While three of the Beatles felt Phil was a savior, Paul hated the new versions, especially of his own songs.

To add insult to injury, Paul was asked to delay the solo album he was releasing. After John left, Paul became a recluse and started recording his own album from his home, playing all the instruments by himself. He was proud of his work and titled the album *McCartney*. What he didn't put together was that the release date he wanted collided with several other releases: *Let It Be*—the album, and the single—and Ringo's solo album *Sentimental Journey*. Paul received a note, handwritten by John and delivered by Ringo, which stated quite simply that *McCartney*'s release date had been pushed to June. Paul lost his temper and verbally attacked Ringo, who returned to Apple and convinced everyone to let Paul have his release date. Tired of fighting, the group relented and *McCartney* was released on April 17. "Let It Be" was released March 6; Ringo's *Sentimental Journey* went out on March 27; and *Let It Be* was released in May.

But for Paul, the damage was done. His ego had had too much, too many consecutive blows: being outnumbered in favor of Allen, having only three songs on the new album, John breaking up the band, and now, attempting to push back his album. Feeling cast aside and forgotten, Paul took revenge from afar. Still a recluse with a wounded ego, he opted to insert a paper interview with his new album, rather than appear in public:

> Q: Do you foresee a time when Lennon-McCartney becomes
>   an active song-writing partnership again?
> A: No.
> Q: Have you plans for live appearances?
> A: No.
> Q: Are you planning a new album or single with the Beatles?
> A: No.
> Q: Do you miss the Beatles and George Martin? [. . .]
> A: No.[9]

Paul sent this, and more similar questions and answers, out along with his album to the press, a week before it was officially released. On April 10, 1970, the headlines rang out loud and clear: "Paul Leaves the Beatles!"

And suddenly, it was all over. Many emotions washed over the band, from relief to terrible sadness, from hope to regret, from freedom to fear; but only one emotion overcame the fans: complete and utter sorrow. There was a death to be mourned: the death of music, of rock 'n' roll, of the idols that had been there for 10 years and defined so much of their lives. Fans clutched the Beatles' albums to their chests and let the tears flow openly.

Just a few weeks later, the bittersweet and aptly named album and film *Let it Be* were released, on May 8 and 13, 1970, respectively. The album went straight to number one and stayed on the charts for a whole year. The film went on to win both an Oscar and a Grammy. It was the end of an era, and the end of the Beatles. But it was just the beginning of the legend.

NOTES

1. Quoted in Philip Norman, *John Lennon: The Life* (New York: Doubleday Canada, 2008), 583.
2. Ibid., 583.
3. Quoted in Philip Norman, *Shout! The Beatles in Their Generation* (New York: Simon & Schuster, 2005), 413.
4. Quoted in Peter Brown and Steven Gaines, *The Love You Make: An Insider's Story of the Beatles* (New York: McGraw-Hill Book Company, 1976), 334.
5. Quoted in Bob Spitz, *The Beatles: A Biography* (New York: Time Warner Books, 2005), 831.
6. Quoted in Norman, *John Lennon*, 604.
7. Quoted in Keith Badman, *The Beatles: Off the Record* (New York: Music Sales Corporation, 2000), 466.
8. Ibid., 479.
9. Quoted in Spitz, *The Beatles*, 853.

Epilogue

They were one the best-selling bands of all time. They shattered all previous records in terms of single sales, album sales, merchandise sales, and ticket sales, as well as spending more weeks on the charts than any other band in history. Never before had the world had such a reaction to a musical group; never before had records been bought up in such quantities, so fast, and very rarely since. Their style, their clothes, their accents, and their personalities came together at just the right time, and the reaction was astronomical. It is hard to sum up what the Beatles meant to the people around them, to music, and to history. Years later, Murray the K, the wild DJ who accompanied the Beatles on their U.S. tours, attempted to try:

> I think the greatest impact the Beatles had on our lives was their attitude. Their music and their attitude said it all for us. . . . With every album the Beatles gave us a 180-degree change. A completely different change, a different sound, a different attitude. They kept changing with us. They kept pace with us. The Beatles inspired a lot of the political and social revolutions that took place, because from a subliminal standpoint, the Beatles represent change. . . . We know them, selfishly, by what they represented in our lives. But they are indeed four lads from Liverpool

with limited education and background who did remarkably well . . . the influence that that they had was the greatest contribution that they made . . . the Beatles had much more of an effect upon us than we realize.[1]

Indeed, four seemingly simple boys from Liverpool defined a musical and social revolution that led a generation to rise up and take its place in history. Yet the more surprising event took place when teenagers of the following decades decided to pick up a Beatles record, or later a Beatles' eight-track, or even later, a Beatles' CD. Indeed, even today, there is something to be said when teenagers of the newest generation scroll through their iPods, and of all the bands in the entire world sitting at their fingertips, they select the Beatles. And sitting on their buses, in their schools, or in the privacy of their bedrooms, the voices of John, Paul, George, and Ringo reach out and move them, with songs that have left behind the constraints of time and place and have moved to a place of universality. Today, in the hearts of so many—from baby boomers to kindergartners from punks with Mohawks and goths clad in black to the suburbs and the still-thriving Bible Belt, from the center of New York City to the edge of the world—the legend and legacy of the Beatles lives on.

John

Shortly after Paul announced the break-up of the group, John and Yoko went to America. John was partaking in a new, innovative therapy that he hoped would help him deal with issues surround his father, his mother, and his fear of abandonment. The therapy was a concept created by Arthur Janov, in California, called Primal Scream Therapy. Arthur had already flown to Tittenhurst Park to stay with John and Yoko and begin the treatment, but he had patients in California he needed to take care of, so John and Yoko went to California to finish. Arthur's theory was that "almost all neurotic behaviour derived from traumas of childhood,"[2] and that in order to deal with the pain, one must react as a little baby would: by screaming.

While many famous artists have been considered crazy, it's assumed that the madness furthered the art. For John, he simply and desperately needed help. His craziness was ruining his life, turning him into a recluse who trusted no one but Yoko, and even then, he was constantly convinced that Yoko was on the verge of leaving him. Arthur worked with John, helping him to realize the issues that caused him the most pain, while Yoko taught John how to scream, how to really scream. John progressed well in the program and had begun dealing with his deeply rooted issues, when the government informed him that he was overstaying his welcome. Though he was not done with his therapy, John and Yoko had to return to London.

John decided he could do the rest of the treatment himself, the way he knew best: with music. He recorded an album during the summer of 1970, which would be called *John Lennon / Plastic Ono Band*. It included deeply personal songs such as "Mother," "Hold On," and "My Mummy's Dead," as well as "God," in which John announced his disbelief in everything except for Yoko and himself. Also on the album was "Working Class Hero," which was banned for use of the world "fucking." The album was released in December of 1970 and moved, slowly but surely, up the charts; however, instead of being out marketing the album, John was mourning. In October, just before John's thirtieth birthday, Yoko had miscarried once again.

In 1971, John released his next solo effort, *Imagine*. On this album was a direct shot at Paul, called "How Do You Sleep?," as well as "Jealous Guy," which looked at the problems he had had with jealousy ever since the day he had met Cynthia, and again with Yoko. There was "Oh My Love," for Yoko, who remained faithfully by his side day and night. The song that is remembered best, however, was called "Imagine." The song is a call to peace, a call to lay down all the things that separate humanity, and "be as one." While the song lacked lyrically in comparison to John's older songs, it was touching, and enjoyed much success, not only at the time, but again after John passed away, and again in 2001 after the events of September 11. Also in 1971, he and Yoko released "Happy Xmas (War Is Over)," which they wrote together, followed by an album called *Sometime in New York City*. During this time, Yoko and John were able to move to New York.

In 1972, John released another song destined to be banned on the radio: "Woman Is the Nigger of the World." John's raging feminism was a fire fanned by Yoko. John hated how Yoko was treated poorly, cast aside, and ignored. Somewhere, Cynthia Lennon shuddered at the irony that her ex-husband—who had once forbidden her from speaking to other men, who had forced her to be a secret kept from fans, and who had treated her as unworthy of his presence—was now a feminist.

John and Yoko's relationship was on the rocks in 1973. He released an album called *Mind Games*, which marked the beginning of their separation. John's sex drive was still as strong as ever, while Yoko was older, and, after four years together, less inclined to keep up. At a party one night, John grabbed a random girl and pulled her into a closet, in front of all the guests, including Yoko. Yoko didn't make a scene at the time, being an open woman, but she was deeply hurt. She suggested John take a trip away, and she would stay in New York. John chose Los Angeles, and Yoko told him to take their assistant, May Pang, along to help him. What transpired was 14 months of pure hedonistic mayhem, as John was finally the bachelor he had never officially been. This period of time is known as "The Lost Weekend."

After over a year of bachelorhood, and an album called *Walls and Bridges,* John lost a bet with Elton John about a song they had recorded and released together, called "Whatever Gets You through the Night." John had bet that it wouldn't make it to number one, but it did. John had to uphold his side of the deal: come onstage at one of Elton's concerts and play a few songs. On November 28, 1974, John took the stage at Madison Square Garden, alongside Elton John. He played "Whatever Gets You through the Night," "Lucy in the Sky with Diamonds," and "I Saw Her Standing There." Yoko was in the crowd and went backstage afterward, where she and John rekindled their relationship after the long hiatus.

John moved back into their apartment at a building called the Dakota, in New York. They made a renewal of their vows and began anew. As a surprise blessing, Yoko became pregnant almost immediately, at age 42. On October 9, John's 35th birthday, Yoko delivered a baby boy, whom they named Sean Taro. John left the music scene to take care of Sean full-time and effectively became a househusband, cooking, cleaning, and spending every waking moment with his wife and son. John became a familiar figure in the neighborhood, strolling with Sean on walks along Central Park. As Sean grew older, John finally began to think of Julian, his other son, with whom he had had little contact since moving to America. He began to fly Julian, now a teenager, over for visits, rekindling their relationship, taking trips, and making music together. It was hard for Julian, who saw how much material wealth his stepbrother had in New York, while he and Cynthia lived a middle-class life back in England. Julian had always felt he was unwanted by his father, an eerie call-back to John's own childhood.

After a four-year hiatus from music, John began work on a new album called *Double Fantasy.* The album was a collaboration between

John and Yoko, writing songs in response to each other. John wrote "I'm Losing You," which matched Yoko's song, "I'm Moving On." John wrote "Beautiful Boy," an ode to Sean, and Yoko wrote "Beautiful Boys," a song for the two men in her life, John and Sean. John worked on *Double Fantasy* through the summer and fall. On October 9, he turned 40. John was busy reinventing himself and taking care of his son, and polishing off a new album. He also had a new single out and doing well, called "(Just Like) Starting Over,"

December 8, 1980, was a day just like any other. John and Yoko had breakfast together, and John had his hair cut short, teddy-boy style, in preparation for a photo shoot for *Rolling Stone Magazine.* At the photo shoot, John wore a leather jacket and blue jeans, with his hair greased up like back in the days of the Cavern or the Kaiserkeller. That day, he and Yoko also gave a long interview with a radio station, RKO Radio. It would be the last interview of his life. "I'm really talking to the people that grew up with me," said John, "I'm saying here I am now. How are you? How's your relationship going? Did you get through it all? Wasn't the 70s a drag? Here we are, well let's try and make the 80s good. . . . We're going into an unknown future, but we're still all here. We're still wild as life. There's hope." His overall tone, just hours before being shot, was positive:

> "I'm so hungry for making records, because of the way I feel. . . . We feel like this is just the start . . . like this is our first album. I feel like nothing happened before today. . . . I consider that my work won't be finished until I'm dead and buried. And I hope that's a long long time."[3]

Earlier that day, a fan had asked John for an autograph. John politely obliged, asking if there was anything else he could do, while a photograph snapped a picture of him and Yoko. In the photo, an aging John Lennon is looking down, concentrating on signing a copy of *Double Fantasy*, with his fan, Mark David Chapman, looking over his shoulder. John Lennon, and his soon-to-be killer, were side by side, on the day of his death.

John spent the evening in the recording studio, when he and Yoko decided to return home to tuck Sean into bed. His limo pulled up at the curb at the Dakota, and as he stepped out onto the sidewalk, he heard someone call his name, quietly. Mark David Chapmen proceeded to shoot John four times with a .38 handgun. John, stunned, staggered into the lobby of the Dakota and collapsed on the floor. Tapes, containing the songs he had been working on, went flying across the floor. Yoko came running in behind him, screaming that he had been shot. He was pronounced dead at 11:07 P.M. Mark David Chapman waited on the sidewalk for the police to show up, thumbing his copy of *The Catcher in the Rye,* inside which he had written "This is my statement."

Thus, one of the most documented and monumental lives of the 21st century came to an end. John was mourned by all who had known him—Yoko, Sean, Paul, George, Ringo, Cynthia, Julian, Aunt Mimi, George Martin, and Neil Aspinall, to name a few—and of course, by fans around the world. If fans thought they had known pain when the Beatles had broken up, then they were ill-prepared to deal with this. People famous for political reasons might have had to worry about being hurt, but never before had celebrities been threatened. Candlelight vigils were held nightly in cities all over the world. John was mourned as if he were a saint, in the same way that people had mourned John Fitzgerald Kennedy, Martin Luther King Jr., or later, Princess Diana. He was a hero, an activist, a brilliant musician, and, at heart, just a young boy from Liverpool with dreams of making it as big as Elvis.

Imagine: Upwards of 100,000 people cram the streets outside John Lennon's apartment building, the Dakota, in New York, to mourn his death. December 14, 1980. (AP Photo/David Bookstaver)

Double Fantasy went number one around the world, including in America and the United Kingdom, and went on to win a Grammy for 1981 Album of the Year. Six months after his death, Yoko released an album called *Seasons of Glass*; its cover was a photo of John's blood-splattered glasses. In 1984, a posthumous album of some songs John had written was released, called *Milk and Honey*, which went to number 3 in the United Kingdom and number 11 in America. In 1986, two other posthumous albums were released: one consisted of various takes from previous albums, compiled and called *Menlove Ave*, after the street where he grew up with his Aunt Mimi; the other was a live concert from 1972, called *Live in New York City*. Most recently, an album called *Acoustic* was released in 2004, consisting of just John and no backing group. In 1988, a full-length documentary about the making of the *Imagine* album was released, to much acclaim, and in 2007 a film depicting John's death was released, called *Chapter 27*, starring Jarred Leto as Mark David Chapman, and, ironically, an actor named Mark Chapman as John Lennon.

In 1987, John was inducted into the Songwriters Hall Of Fame, and then in 1994, he was inducted into the Rock 'n' Roll Hall Of Fame. In 1991, he was awarded the Grammy Lifetime Achievement Award. In 2002, John was voted number 8 on a poll of 100 Greatest Britons, and most recently he ranked number 5 on Rolling Stone's list of 100 Greatest Singers of All Time in 2008.

Many tributes exist for John around the world. In Liverpool, a statue of a young John leans cockily against the wall where the Cavern used to be. There is a memorial garden in Central Park, New York, called "Strawberry Fields." There is a statue of a 1970s-esque John sitting in a park in Havana, Cuba, an Imagine Peace Tower in Iceland, and a John Lennon Museum in Japan. Most touchingly, the airport in Liverpool, formerly known as the Speke Airport, was renamed the Liverpool John Lennon Airport and officially made its motto "Above Us Only Sky."

Each year, on both the day of his birth and the day of his death, fans gather at various locations around the world to celebrate and mourn their fallen hero. But John Lennon lives on. John lives on through his activism and messages, as when, in the dust of the attacks on New York on September 11, 2001, when on October 2, a television special aired, called *Come Together: A Night for John Lennon's Words and Music*, dedicated to those who lost their lives, and as an urging to fellow Americans to consider John's message of peace. John lives in Yoko, as she continues to campaign for peace, to share

John's art and music, and to hold charity events in his name. John lives on in his sons, as both Sean and Julian have enjoyed successful careers in the music industry, though they must live forever in their father's shadow. Most of all, John Lennon lives on in his music, his first, and truest, love.

George

By the time the Beatles broke up, George had released two solo albums: *Wonderwall Music* and *Electronic Sound*, both of which were mainly instrumental. So when the announcement finally went public, George, like John, felt himself finally free of the restraints of the band. Out from under John and Paul's shadows, George struck out on his own and released an onslaught of his own music, which he had been compiling quietly on his own time over the years, and released an unheard-of *triple album*, aptly named *All Things Must Pass*. The first two discs were songs with lyrics, and the third disc was mostly instrumental, consisting of George playing with other artists such as Eric Clapton, Billy Preston, and Ringo. It was well-received both in the United Kingdom and America, and the single, called "My Sweet Lord," went to number one. The album, released November 27, 1970, caught audiences and fans off guard as the "quiet Beatle" stepped into the spotlight. The album went to number one in the United States, Canada, the United Kingdom, and Australia.

In 1971, George signed on for a charity concert, alongside his sitar guru Ravi Shankar, Bob Dylan, Eric Clapton, Billy Preston, and Ringo. The concert was to raise money and awareness for refugees from Bangladesh, who had lost everything either to a cyclone, or the Bangladesh Liberation War, or both. The event was called The Concert for Bangladesh and was recorded and filmed, to be released later as an album and a film—much like *Let It Be*. The actual event took place in Madison Square Garden, with 40,000 people in attendance, on August 1. It was the first charity concert of its kind. The album was released in 1971, and the film came out in 1972, both to much success.

George continued to put out albums, but none of them reached the success of *All Things Must Pass*. In 1973, he released *Living in the Material World*, which did go to number one, but only for a few weeks. One single was released, called "Give Me Love (Give Me Peace on Earth)," which also went to number one in America. The album contained a song called "Sue Me, Sue You Blues," which was a commentary on the last year of the Beatles, and a stab at Allen Klein. However, most of his other songs on the album were highly spiritual and saturated with his Hindu beliefs, which sabotaged its chance at being number one for very long.

In 1974, George and Pattie divorced. Throughout their relationship, George had known that Pattie was astonishingly attractive, the classic '60s girl with huge dark eyes and platinum blond hair, and that his fellow bandmates and friends were attracted to her, such as John Lennon and Mick Jagger. What he had not known, or had chosen to ignore, was the fact that Eric Clapton was head-over-heels in love with Pattie, dating back to the late 1960s when George brought Eric in to play on some tracks. For years, Eric pursued Pattie, even dating her sister in an attempt to curb his passion. While George had written "Something" for Pattie, Eric turned up with a song called "Layla," which was also for her, and effectively stole her heart. Pattie truly loved George, but his obsessive spirituality made him reclusive, and his fame made him promiscuous, the latter being the final straw when Pattie claimed she discovered that George was having an affair with Maureen, Ringo's wife.[4] That year, Pattie left George and began her relationship with Eric, whom she would eventually marry.

This fueled George's next album, *Dark Horse*. The album peaked at number four in the Unites States but was received critically due to the fact that George had had laryngitis during the recording. In 1975, he released *Extra Texture (Read All about It)*, which was supposed to be his last released by EMI, as his contract was expiring, but EMI managed to squeeze one more in, releasing *The Best of George Harrison* just shy the of end of the contract. George then went on to form *Dark Horse Records*, his own record company, and opened an office in Los Angeles. His office was in the same building as A&M Records, where a young woman named Olivia Arias worked. George was taken with Olivia and the two began dating. Four years later, they married and remained married until George passed away, 23 years later.

Dark Horse Records' first release was *Thirty Three & 1/3*, which came out in 1976 and went to number 11 in America and included two singles: "This Song" and "Crackerbox Palace," both of which appeared in the top 25. On this album, George had finally moved away from his overbearing religious lyrics and East Indian sound and returned to playing with melodies, and Westernized lyrics and instruments. After George and Olivia married in 1978, they had a son, whom George named Dhani, after two notes on the Indian scale of music, "dha" and "ni." In 1979, inspired by his new marriage and son,

George released a self-titled album to cap off a decade, *George Harrison*, which enjoyed mild success.

In 1980, George was devastated by the news of John Lennon's death. Though George had played on John's album *Imagine*, the two had drifted apart since, mostly over George's dislike of Yoko. Many arguments later, the two barely ever spoke. Earlier in 1980, George published his autobiography, called *I, Me, Mine,* which had little mention of John. This had deeply hurt John, and the two didn't reconcile in time. George felt deep regret and sorrow over how things ended between them. The month before John died, George, Paul, and Ringo had gotten together to record a song. In an attempt to make amends after John's death, George rewrote the song, added new lyrics, and made it about John, called "All Those Years Ago." The tribute was released in 1981 and went to number two in America, though it was for just a few weeks. The song was released on George's next album, called *Somewhere in England*, which peaked at number 11 in America. George's follow-up album was called *Gone Troppo*, but it received little to no recognition and barely even made a blip on the radar in terms of the charts. George would not make another album for nearly five years.

He reappeared in 1987 with *Cloud Nine,* which had much success, peaking at number 8 in America and number 10 in the United Kingdom. The first single, "Got My Mind Set on You," was a big hit and went to number one in America and number two in the United Kingdom. The second single was a reflection on his time with the Beatles, called "When We Was Fab," which peaked at number 30 in America.

From 1988 to 1990, George recorded alongside a super-group comprising Bob Dylan, Roy Orbison, Tom Petty, and Jeff Lynne, called the Traveling Wilburys. Their first album, *The Traveling Wilburys Vol. 1*, was released in October of 1988. The album went to number 3 in America, and number 16 in the United Kingdom, which was surprising considering the entire album was done with fake names. When Roy Orbison died suddenly that Christmas, the band continued on as a foursome and released their next album, *The Traveling Wilburys Vol. 3*. Though it was only their second album, they dubbed it "Vol. 3" as a joke. It was not as well-received as their first album.

Also during this time, Eric Clapton—who had surprisingly remained one of George's good friends—convinced him to come on a tour to Japan. It would be George's last tour. The footage was later released as an album called *Live in Japan* in 1992.

In 1994, the three remaining Beatles reunited for a project called *The Beatles Anthology*. It consisted of long, in-depth interviews with each of them, as well as the release of a new single. The three of them recorded a song built around some old recorded vocals of John's from 1977, called "Free As a Bird." They also released a music video for the song, which referenced many old Beatles hits, such as "Penny Lane," "Eleanor Rigby," and "Strawberry Fields Forever," and showed various scenes from their time as a band, from the Cavern to Shea Stadium and beyond. Released on November 20, 1995," Free As a Bird" went to number six in America and number 2 in the United Kingdom, making it the first hit the Beatles had had in 26 years.

In 1997, George found a lump on his throat and discovered he had throat cancer from all his years of smoking. He began treatment but also had to battle lung cancer, and a tumor in his brain. After a long battle, George passed away on November 29, 2001. He was cremated, and his ashes were scattered along the Ganges River in India.

In the last years of his life, George had been returning to the recording studio in hopes of putting out another album. As the seriousness of his cancer became apparent, he only worked harder to get the album completed. Unable to finish it before his death, he left instructions for his son, Dhani, to finish it. The album, titled *Brainwashed*, was released in November of 2002 and was well-received, going to number 18 in America and number 29 in the United Kingdom. In 2004, George was inducted into Rock 'n' Roll Hall of Fame for his solo career.

Dhani Harrison went on to perform alongside Eric Clapton, Ravi Shankar, Billy Preston, and Tom Petty, as well as Paul and Ringo, in a tribute concert called *Concert for George*. He also played a large role in the creation of a Beatles video game, *Beatles Rockband*, in 2009. Dhani continues to make music, work on Beatles projects, and oversee rereleases of his father's work. On June 16, 2009, EMI released a compilation of George's best work, called *Let It Roll: Songs by George Harrison*, which went to number four in the United Kingdom, his highest chart position since 1973.

Ringo

Ringo carried on after the break-up without much fuss or drama. In 1970, he welcomed his third child, Lee, into the world, to join his two other children, Zak and Jason. Also that year, as a follow-up to his successful album *Sentimental Journey*, Ringo got back to work and recorded *Beaucoups of Blues*. When that album failed to do well, Ringo began releasing singles on Apple Records and had some hits: in 1971, "It Don't Come Easy," which peaked at number 4 in America; and in 1972, "Back off Boogaloo," which peaked at number 2.

In 1971, Ringo participated in George's *The Concert for Bangladesh*, though both Paul and John declined. In 1973, he released another solo album, *Ringo,* which went to number two in America and had guest appearances by the other three Beatles (although not at the same time). In 1974, he released his fourth album, *Goodnight Vienna*, which had two very successful hits on it: "Photograph," featuring George, and "You're Sixteen," both of which reached number one in America. In 1975, Ringo released his first compilation album of his greatest hits, entitled *Blast from Your Past,* which appeared at number 30 on the American charts, but not at all in the United Kingdom. Sadly, in 1975, Ringo was divorced from Maureen, after 10 years of marriage, having never quite recovered from Maureen's affair with George. In the mid-1970s, Ringo's career began to drop off. In 1975, he started his own record company, much as George had, called Ring O'Records. In 1976, he released *Ringo's Rotogravure*, along with a single, "A Dose of Rock 'n' Roll," which peaked at number 26 in America before vanishing quickly. Ringo attempted another album in 1977, called *Ringo the 4th*, in which Ringo attempted to make disco music. The album was a total bust, failing to go any further than number 162 in America, and it damaged Ringo's reputation as a musician. His only success that year was appearing on a children's album about a mouse from Liverpool who immigrated to America, called *Souse the Mouse*. In 1978, Ringo released another album, *Bad Boy*, in hopes of saving his rapidly fading career, but it too barely made the charts, showing up at number 129 in America.

Ringo was on vacation in the Bahamas when he heard John had been shot. He immediately flew to New York to comfort Yoko and Sean, although he did so quietly, not wanting to bring attention to the family at such a time. Ringo had maintained a good relationship with John over all the years and mourned his death in his own private way.

The same year of John's death, Ringo met a beautiful woman named Barbara Bach on the set of a film called *Caveman*. Barbara had been a model, an actress, and a *Playboy* model and seemed out of Ringo's league; however, she was intrigued and amused by Ringo's quirky personality and the two fell in love. They were married in 1981, attended by Paul and Linda, as well as George and Olivia. That year Ringo returned to the studio again, only to record two more commercial flops, *Stop and Smell the Roses,* and *Old Wave,* even though both Paul and George had helped him on the albums. Even John had tried to help, handing Ringo two songs for *Stop and Smell the Roses* just two weeks before being shot; however, after John's death he felt it was inappropriate to include the songs, especially the ironically titled "Life Begins at 40."

Through the rest of the 1980s, the most success Ringo saw was as the narrator of *Thomas the Tank Engine,* a children's TV show. With the downturn of his career, Ringo took to drowning his sorrows with alcohol, and Barbara joined him. By 1988, the two were full-blown alcoholics and eventually checked themselves into a clinic to get clean. In 1989, feeling refreshed and reborn, Ringo hit the road with his new group, Ringo Starr & His All-Starr Band. Ringo's concept was that each member of the band was a musician in his own right, each member was a star, and therefore concerts consisted of each member having a solo set performing their own personal hits. Similar to John and Yoko's idea of the Plastic Ono Band being flexible with members, the All-Starr Band line-up changed with every tour. Over the years, members consisted of Billy Preston, Burton Cummings, Randy Bachman, Peter Frampton, and his own son, Zak. In 1989, their first performance was in Dallas, Texas, to a crowd of over 10,000 people.

In 1992, Ringo released his supposed come-back album, titled *Time Takes Time.* While he worked with the music industry's top record producers, and although the album received praise for its music, it simply failed to chart, once again. The attempted single, "Weight of the World," peaked at number 72 in America. Ringo tried again in 1998, with *Vertical Man,* which included appearances by Alanis Morissette, Brian Wilson, Ozzy Osbourne, Steven Tyler, and Tom Petty, as well as Paul and George. The album peaked at number 61 in America, and number 85 in the United Kingdom. This album was the first work Ringo did with his new band, the Roundheads.

In 2002, Ringo was inducted into the Percussive Arts Society Hall of Fame; also that year he participated in *Concert for George,* upon the passing of his beloved former band-mate. At the concert, he performed "Photograph" and sang the heartbreaking lyrics "Every time I see your face / it reminds me of the places we used to go," which he had written with George so many years before. It was a sentimental moment, similar to years earlier in 1995, when Paul, George, and Ringo had been interviewing for the *Anthology* series, and Ringo, with a few tears in his eyes, looked at the camera and said that, in the end, the Beatles had just been "four guys who loved each other."[5]

In 2003, Ringo released *Ringo Rama*, which opened with a tribute song to George, titled "Never without You." In 2005, Ringo released *Choose Love*. Both albums failed to chart. *Choose Love* included "Oh My Lord," which was a parody of George's song, "My Sweet Lord." Regardless, EMI decided to release a compilation of Ringo's best work called *Photograph: The Very Best of Ringo Starr,* in August of 2007. In 2008, Ringo released his fourteenth solo album, called *Liverpool 8,* which peaked at number 91 in the United Kingdom and number 94 in America.

Ringo is still married to Barbara, and his three children have had kids of their own, making him a grandfather. Ringo's youngest daughter, Lee, was diagnosed with a brain tumor in 1995 but survived treatment. That same year, however, Maureen was diagnosed with leukemia and passed away in 1996, with her family by her side, Ringo included. In 2001, Lee's tumor returned, but once again she survived treatment. In 2009, Lee announced that she and her boyfriend were expecting triplets.

Zak Starkey made his dad proud when he became the unofficial fill-in drummer for the band the Who in 1994. Keith Moon had been a friend of Ringo's, and an idol to Zak, and it was hugely exciting that Zak got to both record, and tour, with the band. Then in 2004, Zak joined the British group Oasis and toured with them through 2005 and 2006. He continues to make music and carry on his father's legacy.

In 2009, Ringo produced his next album himself, titled *Y Not.* One of the songs, "Walk with You," was written and recorded alongside Paul and is a joyful look at the beauty of lifelong friendships. It is a fitting tune for the two surviving Beatles, having gone through a historic and whirlwind life together. Ringo continues to be the man he has always been: content, optimistic, and hopeful for the future.

Paul

One might think that Paul had more pressing matters to tend to when the Beatles broke up: most notably, the "fact" that he was dead. In 1969, an American radio DJ named Russell Gibb went on the air to announce the news that Paul McCartney had died in 1966, and that evidence of this was strewn through their music and movies ever since. Russell claimed a man who identified himself only as "Tom" had called him and informed him of this. When Russell took it public, a surprising amount of fans ate it up, addicted and obsessed with the "clues" found in Beatles' songs, and the conspiracy theory grew to heights no one expected.

The theory is based on the idea that Paul died in 1966 in a terrible car accident. Supposedly, this occurred at 5 A.M., on Wednesday, November 9, 1966. Various lyrics pointed crazed fans to this date: the lines "He blew his mind out in a car / He didn't notice the light had changed," from "A Day In the Life," showed that Paul was driving and entered an intersection after the light had turned red; in the same song, and again in "Revolution #9," sound effects of a car accident are apparent in the background; from the song "She's Leaving Home," the lyric "Wednesday morning at 5 o'clock as the day begins," pointed fans to both the time, and day of the week of the accident; and "Wednesday morning papers didn't come," from the song "Lady Madonna," apparently hinted at the fact that the other Beatles concealed the disaster and hid the news from the daily papers.

The album that would have come out after Paul's supposed death was *Sgt. Pepper*. The clues on the album cover proved worthy of the conspiracy. For example, the unearthed soil under the flowers appears to be a freshly filled grave, with the drum standing in place of a gravestone. The drum itself is another clue: when a mirror is place right down the middle of the words "Lonely Hearts," the image reads "1 ONE 1 X HE DIE." The "1 ONE 1 X" references the three surviving Beatles, and one dead, while "HE DIE," is below Paul, along with a little arrow pointing at him. This little clue is also where the exact date of November 9 comes from, with "1 ONE" being 11, or the 11th month, and "1X" being the Roman numeral for 9; hence, November 9, which also happened to be a Wednesday, as pointed to in the aforementioned songs, in 1966. While nearly every image on the cover was analyzed, the most disturbing and obvious image was the open palm above Paul's head, a symbol of death in Indian culture. Also, on the back of the album and in photos throughout, Paul faces away while the other three face forward. As for the lyrics, the most notable was in the first song, "Sgt. Pepper," where the character "Billy Shears" is introduced. After Paul was reputed to have died in the car accident, the Beatles had supposedly held a look-alike contest, and the man that won was named William Shears Campbell, a.k.a. Billy.

While nearly all the Beatles' albums have been combed through with impeccable detail searching for clues (and indeed, to whoever believes, hundreds and hundreds of clues are available), the other album with the most steadfast clues, after *Sgt. Pepper*, is *Abbey Road*. The most common interpretation was that John was the priest, or holy person, dressed all in white and leading the precession, while Ringo, clad in black, was a mourner; next was Paul, walking barefoot, representing a person about to be buried, as was the custom, and finally George, dressed in jeans, to represent the gravedigger. Other clues included the license plate of the Beetle car, reading "28IF," alluding to the fact that Paul would be 28 if he were alive, and that Paul is stepping out of sync with the other Beatles, leading with his left leg, while the other three lead with their right. Finally, Paul is smoking with his right hand, when he was known to be left-handed, thus somehow proving that it was really Paul's stand-in, Billy Shears.

Aside from album covers, lyrics were the best clues. Fanatics began playing albums backward, desperately searching for clues, which, of course, they managed to find. There are many lists of lyrics that have alternative messages when played backward, but the interpretation seems to depend on the ear of the one listening. On "Revolution #9," when the lyric "number nine" is played backward, it says "turn me on, dead man"; and on "Let It Be," "let it be" backward sounds like "he's dead." Most famous was on "All Together Now," where John sings "all together now," over and over again, but backward he sings "I buried Paul." This also shows up at the end of "Strawberry Fields Forever"; just as the song is fading out, John mumbles "I buried Paul." In an interview, Paul attempted to clear things up: "At the end of 'Strawberry Fields' that wasn't 'I buried Paul' at all. That was John saying 'Cranberry Sauce.' That's John's humor."[6] In the end, most people probably hear whatever they want to.

All of this caused a wave of publicity about Paul, and his supposed death. Paul gave interview after interview stating over and over again that he was alive and well, but the conspiracy seemed to have a life of its own. The conspiracy slowed down for a bit after the break-up but reappeared in 1979 when more in-depth "research" went public, and more "clues" were found. Paul carried on with his life, but the "Paul is Dead" campaigned followed him wherever he went. It has been parodied in song, on television, and in movies.

In reality, after beating John to the punch line and announcing the break-up that was never his, Paul continued to be a recluse (which only furthered the "Paul is dead" rumors). He and Linda, along with Heather and their new baby Mary, went to Paul's farm in Scotland and attempted to disappear for a while. He released *McCartney,* on which he played every instrument himself, and it went straight to number one in America and number two in the United Kingdom. The album included a song called "Maybe I'm Amazed," a love song for Linda, which was never officially released as a single but enjoyed success as the best song on an otherwise mediocre album.

In 1971, Paul and Linda released *Ram*, a supposedly collaborative effort that featured mostly Paul with Linda on backing vocals. The album was also a success, going to number one in the United Kingdom and number two in America. *Ram* included a song called "Too Many People," which John took as a shot at himself and Yoko, and to which John later responded to with "How Do You Sleep?" On the back of *Ram* there was a photo of two beetles copulating, which might be a picture of how Paul felt he was being treated at the time. No singles were released from the album; however, Paul recorded a nonalbum single called "Another Day," which had great success around the world.

By the fall of 1971, Paul had a new band, a new album, and a new baby. The band was called Wings and comprised himself, Linda, Denny Seiwell, a drummer, and Denny Laine, a guitarist. Wings would go on to be the only post-Beatle band to enjoy long-term success, with every one of their 23 singles going into the top 40, and all of their nine albums entering the top 10 in either America or the United Kingdom. The band would go through several different lineups, but it always included both Paul and Linda. Their first album was called *Wild Life*, which went to number 11 in the United Kingdom, and number 10 in America. Also at this time, Paul and Linda gave birth to their second baby, Stella.

By early 1972, the band had added another guitarist, an Irishman named Henry McCollough. With Paul having Irish roots, and McCollough joining the group, the band recorded a protest song against the events taking place in Northern Ireland, namely, "Bloody Sunday," where nearly 30 activists were shot during a North Ireland Civil Rights Association march, 14 of whom died. The song was called "Give Ireland Back to the Irish," which, although it was banned from the radio, went to number 16 in the United Kingdom and number 1 in the Republic of Ireland.

In response to being banned, the group cheekily released a new single, which was a cover of "Mary Had a Little Lamb." Surprisingly, it entered the top 10 in the United Kingdom. Following that, they released "Hi, Hi, Hi," which was banned from the radio for questionable lyrics involving drug use. Later in 1972, they recorded the theme song for a new James Bond movie, "Live and Let Die," to go with the movie of the same name. It was a hit around the world and went on to be covered by many other artists.

Their second album was *Red Rose Speedway*, in 1973, though the name of the band changed briefly to Paul McCartney and Wings. This album contained Wings' first number-one hit, "My Love." Soon afterward they put out their next album, called *Band on the Run*. Oddly, the album was mixed in Lagos, Nigeria; regardless, it went to number one in both the United Kingdom and America.

In 1975, Wings released their next album, *Venus and Mars*. During this time, the Wings lineup began to change, with various members coming and going. This album contained another number-one hit, "Listen to What the Man Said." With such success in their wake, the band decided to embark on a world tour, called Wings over the World. In 1976, they released *Wings at the Speed of Sound*, which bore them two number-one singles in America: "Silly Love Songs," and "Let Me In." Also in 1976, they released a triple record of songs recorded during their world tour, called *Wings over America*, which would become their fifth album to hit number one. Just in time for Christmas, Paul released "Mull of Kintyre," an ode to the place where his farm was, and it became the only song by Wings to hit number one in the United Kingdom. In 1977, Paul and Linda had their third child, a boy named James.

In 1978, Wings released *London Town*, which marked Paul's transition into the use of synthesizers, followed by *Back to the Egg* in 1979, the latter being Wings's last studio album. Neither were well well-received by critics, but they sold well and entered the top 10. *Back to the Egg* featured a jam session called "Rockestra Theme," which was a recording session that included members of Pink Floyd, Led Zeppelin, and the Who. The song enjoyed much success and a Grammy award.

In early 1980, Paul was busted for possession of marijuana at an airport in Japan. Paul was arrested, and the Wings tour of Japan was canceled. Paul stayed in jail for nine whole days before being released and sent back to England. Upon his return, he put Wings on hold and began recording his own music, back on his farm in Scotland. Paul released *McCartney II*, his first solo album in 10 years, which featured more synthesizers and other studio experimentation; regardless, the album went to number one in the United Kingdom and number 3 in America.

In the fall of 1980, Paul returned to the recording studio with Wings; however, when Paul found out that John had been shot, he was too devastated to continue. Both the album, and the band, was abandoned for the time being. Despite their grievances, John and Paul had been best friends since high school and had gone through more together in 10 years than most would in several lifetimes. Though they had not spoken or kept in touch, and though they each had a disregard for the other's music, they were inextricably connected. With John dead, Paul was missing a part of himself.

Two months after John's death, Paul went back to the studio to finish off the album that Wings had started; but this time, he did it alone. The album was named *Tug of War*, a metaphor for his and John's relationship, and was a tribute to his long-time friend and musical soulmate. It was released in 1982 to instant success around the world. Paul went on to release a slew of solo albums: *Pipes of Peace* in 1983, *Give My Regards to Broad Street* in 1984 (which went to number one in America), *Press to Play* in 1986, and *Flowers in the Dirt* in 1988 (which went to number one in America as well). All of the albums entered the top 20, with more success in America than in the United Kingdom. Also, in 1985 Paul participated in the first-ever Live Aid, a benefit for the famine in Ethiopia, which consisted of two massive live concerts (attended by nearly 100,000 people each), raising hundreds of millions of dollars for the cause.

The 1990s saw Paul beginning to slow down, releasing only one album during the first seven years, called *Off the Ground*, in 1993. While touring for *Off the Ground*, he taped a show in Australia and released it as a live album, called *Paul Is Live*, a direct call-back to the "Paul Is Dead" theory. On the album of *Paul Is Live*, Paul is shown crossing Abbey Road once again, but this time all the supposed "clues" had been corrected: Paul is wearing shoes, leading with his left leg, walking his dog with his left hand, and the license plate on the Beetle car reads "51 IS."

In 1997, he was knighted for services to music and became Sir Paul McCartney. With the spotlight back on him, he released a new album in 1997, called *Flaming Pie*, which went to number two in both the United Kingdom and America. The following year, in 1998, his beloved Linda succumbed to breast cancer and passed away, just shy of their thirtieth anniversary.

In 1999, Paul was inducted into the Rock 'n' Roll Hall of Fame and released another solo effort, *Run Devil Run*, but it didn't do as well as he hoped, peaking at only number 12 in America, and number 27 in the United Kingdom. In 2001, he released *Driving Rain*, but it too let him down, peaking at only number 46 in America and number 26 in the United Kingdom. That year, George passed away, leaving Paul once again devastated. The two had rekindled their partnership for the filming of the *Anthology* series in the mid-1990s.

In 2002, Paul participated in *Concert for George*, as a tribute to his friend.

Gathering all the strength and creativity he could, he tried again in 2005 and released *Chaos and Creation in the Backyard*, which was highly successful. The album peaked at number 10 in America and number 6 in the United Kingdom, effectively resurrecting Paul as a musical force. His success was aided by the release of *Love* in 2006, a soundtrack of remixed Beatles' music, which accompanied a theatrical Cirque Du Soleil show. The album went to number one around the world, and Cirque Du Soleil's *Love* is still performing in Las Vegas, with great success. In 2007, still riding the success of his last album, he released *Memory Almost Full*, which did even better than hoped, peaking at number five in America and number three in the United Kingdom, making it Paul's highest-charting album in years.

In July of 2009, going almost full circle, Paul returned to the stage of *The Ed Sullivan Show*, after nearly 45 years. In November of 2009, a film documenting Paul's triumphant return to New York City's Shea Stadium, now called Citi Field, was released, titled *Good Evening New York City*. Reminiscent of Paul's dream for *Let It Be*, he performed several live shows, which were recorded and released as a movie and an album, finally done right.

On September 9, 2009, *The Beatles: Remastered* box set was released, which contained every album the Beatles had put out, remastered on high-quality recording equipment, giving new life to all their music. The box set also contained documentaries and previously unreleased versions of songs. Four decades after their break-up, the Beatles continue to sell music in huge numbers, with the *Remastered* set scoring rave reviews and selling out in stores around the world. In the wake of this, *Beatles Rockband*, the video game, was released, also to highly acclaimed reviews and large numbers of sales. Both Paul and Ringo are busy giving interviews about the box set, the video game, and their newest albums. The Beatles continue to capture and recapture hearts around the world, with a legacy and legend that only seems to get stronger, more unbelievable, and more sensational as the years go by.

NOTES

1. Quoted in David Pritchard and Alan Lysaght, *The Beatles: An Oral History*. (Toronto: Soddart Publishing, 1998), 317.
2. Quoted in Philip Norman, *John Lennon: The Life* (New York: Doubleday Canada, 2008), 639.

3. Transcribed from video.

4. Pattie Boyd, "My Hellish Love Triangle with George and Eric." *The Daily Mail,* August 6, 2007, http://www.dailymail.co.uk/femail/article-473206/Pattie-Boyd-My-hellish-love-triangle-George-Eric—art-Two.html.

5. Quoted in Philip Norman, *Shout! The Beatles in Their Generation* (New York: Simon & Schuster, 2005), 252.

6. Quoted in Keith Badman, *The Beatles: Off the Record* (New York: Music Sales Corporation, 2000), 265.

Albums

1963

Please Please Me
Label: Parlophone (U.K.)
Released: March 22, 1963

With the Beatles
Label: Parlophone (U.K.)
Released: November 22, 1963

Beatlemania! With the Beatles
Label: Capitol Canada
Released: November 25, 1963

1964

Introducing . . . the Beatles
Label: Vee-Jay (U.S.)
Released: January 10, 1964

Meet the Beatles!
Label: Capitol (U.S.)
Released: January 20, 1964

Twist and Shout
Label: Capitol Canada
Released: February 3, 1964

The Beatles' Second Album
Label: Capitol (U.S.)
Released: April 10, 1964

The Beatles' Long Tall Sally
Label: Capitol Canada
Released: May 11, 1964

A Hard Day's Night
Label: United Artists (U.S.)
Released: June 26, 1964

A Hard Day's Night
Label: Parlophone (U.K.)
Released: July 10, 1964

Something New
Label: Capitol (U.S.)
Released: July 20, 1964

Beatles for Sale
Label: Parlophone (U.K.)
Released: December 4, 1964

Beatles '65
Label: Capitol (U.S.)
Released: December 15, 1964

1965

Beatles VI
Label: Capitol (U.S.)
Released: June 14, 1965

Help!
Label: Parlophone (U.K.)
Released: August 6, 1965

Help!
Label: Capitol (U.S.)
Released: August 13, 1965

Rubber Soul
Label: Parlophone (U.K.)
Released: December 3, 1965

Rubber Soul
Label: Capitol (U.S.)
Released: December 6, 1965

1966

"Yesterday"... and Today
Label: Capitol (U.S.)
Released: June 15, 1966

Revolver
Label: Parlophone (U.K.)
Released: August 5, 1966

Revolver
Label: Capitol (U.S.)
Released: August 8, 1966

1967

Sgt. Pepper's Lonely Hearts Club Band
Label: Parlophone (U.K.), Capitol (U.S.)
Released: June 1, 1967

Magical Mystery Tour
Label: Capitol (U.S.), Parlophone (U.K.)
Released: November 27, 1967

1968

The Beatles
Label: Parlophone (U.K.), Capitol (U.S.)
Released: November 22, 1968

1969

Yellow Submarine
Label: Capitol (U.S.), Parlophone (U.K.)
Released: January 13, 1969

Abbey Road
Label: Parlophone (U.K.), Capitol (U.S.)
Released: September 26, 1969

1970

Let It Be
Label: Parlophone (U.K.), United Artists (U.S.)
Released: May 8, 1970

1973

The Beatles: 1962–1966
Label: Parlophone (U.K.), Capitol (U.S.)
Released: April 19, 1973

The Beatles: 1967–1970
Label: Parlophone (U.K.), Capitol (U.S.)
Released: April 19, 1973

1976

Rock 'n' Roll Music
Label: Capitol (U.S.), Parlophone (U.K.)
Released: June 7, 1976

1977

The Beatles at the Hollywood Bowl
Label: Capitol (U.S.), Parlophone (U.K.)
Released: May 4, 1977

Love Songs
Label: Capitol (U.S.), Parlophone (U.K.)
Released: October 21, 1977

1978

The Beatles Collection
Label: Parlophone (U.K.), Capitol (U.S.)
Released: November 2, 1978

Rarities
Label: Parlophone (U.K.)
Released: December 2, 1978

1980

Rarities
Label: Capitol (U.S.)
Released: March 24, 1980

The Beatles' Ballads
Label: Parlophone (U.K.), Capitol Canada
Released: October 13, 1980

Rock 'n' Roll Music, Volume One
Label: Parlophone (U.K.), Capitol (U.S.)
Released: October 27, 1980

Rock 'n' Roll Music, Volume Two
Label: Parlophone (U.K.), Capitol (U.S.)
Released: October 27, 1980

The Beatles Box
Label: Parlophone (U.K.)
Released: November 3, 1980

1982

Reel Music
Label: Capitol (U.S.), Parlophone (U.K.)
Released: March 22, 1982

20 Greatest Hits
Label: Capitol (U.S.), Parlophone (U.K.)
Released: October 11, 1982

1984

The Early Tapes of the Beatles
Label: Polydor (U.K.)
Released: December 10, 1984

1988

Past Masters, Volume One
Label: Parlophone (U.K.), Capitol (U.S.)
Released: March 7, 1988

Past Masters, Volume Two
Label: Parlophone (U.K.), Capitol (U.S.)
Released: March 7, 1988

Past Masters, Volumes One and Two
Label: Capitol (U.S.), Parlophone (U.K.)
Released: October 24, 1988

The Beatles Box Set
Label: Parlophone (U.K.), Capitol (U.S.)
Released: November 15, 1988

1994

Live at the BBC
Label: Parlophone (U.K.), Capitol (U.S.)
Released: November 30, 1994

1995

Anthology 1
Label: Parlophone (U.K.), Capitol (U.S.)
Released: November 21, 1995

1996

Anthology 2
Label: Parlophone (U.K.), Capitol (U.S.)
Released: March 18, 1996

Anthology 3
Label: Parlophone (U.K.), Capitol (U.S.)
Released: October 28, 1996

1999

Yellow Submarine Songtrack
Label: Parlophone (U.K.), Capitol (U.S.)
Released: September 13, 1999

2000

1
Label: Parlophone (U.K.), Capitol (U.S.)
Released: November 13, 2000

2003

Let It Be...Naked
Label: Parlophone (U.K.), Capitol (U.S.)
Released: November 17, 2003

2004

The Capitol Albums, Volume 1
Label: Capitol (U.S.)
Released: November 16, 2004

2006

The Capitol Albums, Volume 2
Label: Capitol (U.S.)
Released: April 11, 2006

Love
Label: Parlophone (U.K.), Capitol (U.S.)
Released: November 20, 2006

2009

The Beatles in Mono
Label: Parlophone (U.K.), Capitol (U.S.)
Released: September 9, 2009

Mono Masters
Label: Parlophone (U.K.), Capitol (U.S.)
Released: September 9, 2009

The Beatles Stereo Box Set

Label: Parlophone (U.K.), Capitol (U.S.)
Released: September 9, 2009

Past Masters

Label: Parlophone (U.K.), Capitol (U.S.)
Released: September 9, 2009

Singles

The Beatles Years

U.K. Singles

1962

"My Bonnie" / "The Saints"
"Love Me Do" / "P.S. I Love You"

1963

"Please Please Me" / "Ask Me Why"
"From Me to You" / "Thank You Girl"
"She Loves You" / "I'll Get You"
"I Want to Hold Your Hand" / "This Boy"

1964

"Can't Buy Me Love" / "You Can't Do That"
"Ain't She Sweet" / "If You Love Me, Baby"
"A Hard Day's Night" / "Things We Said Today"
"I Feel Fine" / "She's a Woman"

1965

"Ticket to Ride" / "Yes It Is"
"Help!" / "I'm Down"
"Day Tripper" / "We Can Work It Out"

1966

"Paperback Writer" / "Rain"
"Yellow Submarine" / "Eleanor Rigby"

1967

"Penny Lane" / "Strawberry Fields Forever"
"All You Need Is Love" / "Baby, You're a Rich Man"
"Hello, Goodbye" / "I Am the Walrus"

1968

"Lady Madonna" / "The Inner Light"
"Hey Jude" / "Revolution"

1969

"Get Back" / "Don't Let Me Down"
"The Ballad of John and Yoko" / "Old Brown Shoe"
"Something" / "Come Together"

1970

"Let It Be" / "You Know My Name (Look Up the Number)"

The Beatles Years

U.S. Singles

1963

"Please Please Me" / "Ask Me Why"
"From Me to You" / "Thank You Girl"
"She Loves You" / "I'll Get You"
"I Want to Hold Your Hand" / "I Saw Her Standing There"

1964

"Twist and Shout" / "There's a Place"
"Can't Buy Me Love" / "You Can't Do That"
"Do You Want to Know a Secret" / "Thank You Girl"
"A Hard Day's Night" / "I Should Have Known Better"
"I'll Cry Instead" / "I'm Happy Just to Dance with You"
"And I Love Her" / "If I Fell"
"I Feel Fine" / "She's a Woman"

1965

"Eight Days a Week" / "I Don't Want to Spoil the Party"
"Ticket to Ride" / "Yes It Is"

"Help!" / "I'm Down"
"Yesterday" / "Act Naturally"
"We Can Work It Out" / "Day Tripper"

1966

"Nowhere Man" / "What Goes On"
"Paperback Writer" / "Rain"
"Yellow Submarine" / "Eleanor Rigby"

1967

"Penny Lane" / "Strawberry Fields Forever"
"All You Need Is Love" / "Baby, You're a Rich Man"
"Hello, Goodbye" / "I Am the Walrus"

1968

"Lady Madonna" / "The Inner Light"
"Hey Jude" / "Revolution"

1969

"Get Back" / "Don't Let Me Down"
"The Ballad of John and Yoko" / "Old Brown Shoe"
"Something" / "Come Together"

1970

"Let It Be" / "You Know My Name (Look Up the Number)"
"The Long and Winding Road" / "For You Blue"

Post-Beatles

1976

"Yesterday" / "I Should Have Known Better"
"Got to Get You into My Life" / "Helter Skelter"
"Back in the U.S.S.R." / "Twist and Shout"
"Ob-La-Di, Ob-La-Da" / "Julia"

1978

"Sgt. Pepper's Lonely Hearts Club Band" / "With a Little Help from My Friends" / "A Day in the Life"

1982

"The Beatles Movie Medley" / "I'm Happy Just to Dance with You"

1995

"Baby It's You" / "I'll Follow the Sun" / "Devil in Her Heart" / "Boys"

"Free as a Bird" / "Christmas Time (Is Here Again)"

1996

"Real Love" / "Baby's in Black"

Awards

The Grammy Awards

1966 Best New Artist—The Beatles
1966 Best Performance by a Vocal Group—"A Hard Day's Night"
1666 Song of the Year—"Michelle"
1966 Best Contemporary Pop Vocal Performance, Male—Paul McCartney, "Eleanor Rigby"
1968 Album of the Year—*Sgt. Pepper*
1968 Best Contemporary Album—*Sgt. Pepper*
1968 Best Album Cover—*Sgt. Pepper*
1968 Best Engineered Recording, Non Classical—*Sgt. Pepper*
1970 Best Original Score for a Motion Picture—*Let It Be*
1972 Grammy Trustees Award—The Beatles
1975 Hall of Fame—The Beatles
1989 Lifetime Achievement Award—Paul McCartney
1990 Lifetime Achievement Award—John Lennon
1997 Best Music Video, Long Form—*The Beatles Anthology*
1997 Best Music Video, Short Form—"Free As a Bird"
1997 Best Pop Performances by a Duo or Group with Vocal—"Free As a Bird"
2004 Hall of Fame—George Harrison

2007   Best Surround Sound Album—The Beatles, *Love*

2007   Best Compilation Soundtrack Album for Motion Picture, Television or Other Visual Media—*Love*

Academy Awards

1970   Best Original Score—*Let It Be*

World Music Awards

2001   World's Best Selling Pop/Rock Group—The Beatles

BRIT Awards

1977   Best British Album—*Sgt. Pepper*

1977   Best British Group—The Beatles

1983   Outstanding Contribution—The Beatles

Rock 'n' Roll Hall of Fame

1988   The Beatles

1994   John Lennon

1999   Paul McCartney

1999   George Martin

2004   George Harrison

National Academy of Recording Arts and Sciences Grammy Hall of Fame

1993   The Beatles—*Sgt. Pepper's Lonely Hearts Club Band*

1995   The Beatles—*Abbey Road*

1997   The Beatles—"Yesterday"

1998   The Beatles—"I Want to Hold Your Hand"

1999   The Beatles—*Revolver*; The Beatles—"Strawberry Fields Forever"; John Lennon—"Imagine"

2000   The Beatles—*Rubber Soul*; The Beatles—*A Hard Day's Night*; The Beatles—*The Beatles (The White Album)*

2001   The Beatles—"Hey Jude"; The Beatles, *Meet the Beatles*

2002   The Beatles—"Eleanor Rigby"

2004   The Beatles—"Let It Be"

2008   The Beatles—"Help!"

Further Reading

Badman, Keith. *Beatles: Off the Record*. New York: Music Sales Corporation, 2000.

The Beatles: The Official Web Site. Apple Corps Ltd. http://www.thebeatles.com/.

The Beatles Anthology, DVD. Directed by Bob Smeaton and Geoff Wonfor. London: Apple Corps, 1995.

The Beatles Ultimate Experience: The Beatles Interview Database. http://www.beatlesinterviews.org/.

Brown, Peter, and Steven Gaines. *The Love You Make: An Insider's Story of the Beatles*. New York: McGraw-Hill Book Company, 1976.

Lennon, Cynthia. *John*. New York: Random House, 2005.

Norman, Philip. *John Lennon: The Life*. New York: Doubleday Canada, 2008.

Norman, Philip. *Shout! The Beatles in Their Generation*. New York: Simon & Schuster, 2005.

Pritchard, David, and Alan Lysaght. *The Beatles: An Oral History*. Toronto: Soddart Publishing, 1998.

Spitz, Bob. *The Beatles: The Biography*. Boston: Little, Brown and Company, 2005.

Turner, Steve. *A Hard Day's Write, the Stories behind Every Beatles Song*. New York: Harper Paperbacks, 2005.

Index

About the Author

KATE SIOBHAN MULLIGAN was born and raised in Vancouver, Canada. She has a BFA in Creative Writing from the University of British Columbia, with a focus of nonfiction. She writes for various newspapers around Vancouver, doing concert and music reviews, as well as travel pieces and memoirs. She grew up in a musical home, with a father who was a radio DJ in the 1960s (a job which allowed him to meet nearly all the major musical figures of the era—he even attended the opening of Apple Corps!) so she has a deep and well-bred passion for music. The first song she ever heard by the Beatles was "Love Me Do," and the only CD she listened to as a child was *The Beatles Greatest Hits*. She still resides in her hometown, with her husband Pete, whom she married while writing this book, and their orange cat, Dexter (whom she nearly named "Sgt. Pepper").